CW00584692

British Monsters
Volume Two

15 Terrifying Tales of Britain's
Most Horrific Serial Killers

Robert Keller

Please Leave Your Review of This Book At
http://bit.ly/kellerbooks

ISBN-13: 978-1535211123
ISBN-10: 1535211121

© 2016 by Robert Keller

robertkellerauthor.com

All rights reserved.

No part of this publication may be copied or reproduced in any format, electronic or otherwise, without the prior, written consent of the copyright holder and publisher. This book is for informational and entertainment purposes only and the author and publisher will not be held responsible for the misuse of information contain herein, whether deliberate or incidental.

Much research, from a variety of sources, has gone into the compilation of this material. To the best knowledge of the author and publisher, the material contained herein is factually correct. Neither the publisher, nor author will be held responsible for any inaccuracies.

Table of Contents

Thomas Neill Cream

The Lambeth Poisoner

It was 1892, four years since the deadly psychopath, known only as Jack the Ripper, had killed the last of his five victims. The Ripper had not been forgotten, though, his horrendous crimes lived on in the memory, and speculations as to his identity were still a popular topic of conversation. Yet, even as the Ripper continued to cast his pall over London's East End, another ghoul appeared to prey on the city's streetwalkers. In many ways, this new fiend was more sadistic, more frightening, than the Ripper. Whereas Saucy Jack's kills were executed quickly, by strangulation or the flash of a blade, this brute's hapless victims were consigned to the agonizing death of strychnine poisoning. His name was Dr. Thomas Neill Cream. Some believe he may also have been the elusive Jack.

Thomas Neill Cream was born in Glasgow, Scotland, on May 27, 1850, the first of William and Mary Cream's eight children. Four years after his birth, the family immigrated to Canada and settled in Wolfe's Cove, Quebec. Here, William Cream found employment as a manager with Gilmour & Company, a shipbuilding and lumber firm. Years later, William used his acquired knowledge to start his own lumber business, which prospered. All of the Cream offspring followed their father into this trade, except Thomas who displayed little interest in commerce. An excellent student with a sharp intellect, Thomas decided early on that he wanted to be a doctor. He realized this ambition in April 1876, graduating from the reputable McGill University.

The ink had hardly dried on Cream's diploma when he was in trouble. During his internship, he'd been courting a teenaged girl by the name of Flora Brooks, the daughter of a wealthy hotel owner. When Flora became ill after a visit from Cream, a doctor was called and his examination determined that the young girl had recently had an abortion. The Brooks clan was enraged. They hunted Cream down and forced him to "do the right thing" and marry Flora. Left with no option, Cream went through with the nuptials. But he didn't stick around long. On the morning after the wedding, he was gone, fled to London, England.

Cream arrived in London in October 1876. As a foreign-qualified doctor, he was required to undergo certification before being allowed to practice medicine in Britain. To this extent he registered at St. Thomas' Hospital, in Lambeth, south London, to undergo further training. However, after six months of study, Cream failed to pass the entrance exam at the Royal College of Surgeons, due in the main to his extra-curricular activities. Cream spent more time escorting various society ladies around town than at his studies. He also enjoyed visiting the East End's many taverns, brothels, music halls and vaudeville theaters.

But if Cream wanted to earn a living as a doctor in Britain, he needed to buckle down and pass his examinations. He, therefore, removed himself from the temptations of London and relocated to Edinburgh where he received the requisite qualification from the Royal College of Physicians and Surgeons. Before departing London, though, Cream had had news from his homeland. His wife, Flora, had died, apparently of consumption. Later, a more sinister explanation would surface for Flora's untimely death. It would emerge that she'd died after swallowing some pills that her errant husband had sent her from England.

With certification in hand from the Royal College, Cream was now free to commence his medical career in Britain. However, for some inexplicable reason, he returned to Canada in late 1878 and set up practice in the bustling town of London, Ontario. The practice, on Dundas Street, quickly picked up a solid roster of patients and appeared to be doing well until it was embroiled in scandal. In May 1879, a patient named Kate Gardener was found dead in a shack behind the surgery. An examination revealed that the unmarried woman was pregnant at the time of her death, and it was surmised that she'd come to Dr. Cream for an abortion.

Under questioning, Cream admitted that that was indeed the case but insisted that he had refused to perform the operation. As the corpse had reeked of chloroform, he suggested that Gardner might have killed herself. The inquest, however, rejected that hypothesis and ruled the death a murder. The implication, of course, was that Cream was the culprit and although there was nothing to connect him with the crime, the scandal ruined both his reputation and his medical practice. Before long he'd absconded for Chicago.

Cream arrived in Illinois in August 1879, setting up business at
434 West Madison, conveniently close to the red light district. He
quickly gained a reputation as an abortionist. In early 1880, he
narrowly escaped jail time after a prostitute named Mary Anne
Faulkner was found dead in a tenement flat, the result of a botched
termination. Fortunately for Cream, his politically connected
lawyer managed to get the charges dropped. He also got Cream off
after another patient died as a result of taking one of his
strychnine-laced anti-pregnancy pills.

In addition to his abortion business, Cream made a tidy sum from
quack medicines. One of his most popular remedies was an elixir
claiming to cure epilepsy. A number of patients swore by this
treatment. One of them, a man named Daniel Stott, made the
mistake of sending his attractive young wife to Cream's surgery for
regular doses of the drug. Soon, Cream and Julia Stott were lovers
and when her husband became suspicious of the affair, Cream
doctored his medication with strychnine. Stott died on June 14,
1881, and Cream would likely have gotten away with the murder
had it not been for his own paranoia.

Afraid that the cause of death might be discovered, Cream wrote a
letter to the coroner, accusing the pharmacist of adding strychnine
to his formula. The accusation was passed on to the district
attorney who ordered Stott's body exhumed. As Cream had
attested, large doses of strychnine were found in the man's
stomach - but it was Cream, not the pharmacist, who was blamed.
Hearing of a warrant for his arrest, he fled to Canada but was soon
captured.

Cream was returned to Chicago to stand trial. And with Julia Stott turning state's evidence, he was found guilty of murder. In November 1881, he was sent to Joliet State Penitentiary for life. He'd spend a decade there before being paroled on July 21, 1891, thanks to his brother Daniel's political connections and a considerable sum of money to grease the palms of corrupt state officials.

Cream returned to Canada where a sizeable inheritance of $16,000, left at his father's passing, awaited. Ten years behind bars had taken its toll on the once handsome doctor. He looked older than his forty years, his head bald, skin weathered, eyes watery, yellowed and somewhat crossed. His once trim, square-shouldered build had drooped. He complained of throbbing headaches and spoke with an odd rattle. Prison had changed his attitude too, especially about women who he disparaged at every opportunity. His family was only too happy to bid him farewell when he departed Canada in September 1891 aboard the SS Teutonic bound for Liverpool.

Cream was back in London by October 1891, staying first at Anderson's Hotel on Fleet Street before moving to a first-floor apartment at 103 Lambeth Palace Road, not far from St. Thomas' Hospital. He'd lived in the same area during his previous stay in the city over a decade earlier and it hadn't changed much. Lambeth was still a slum of damp, narrow streets, run-down apartments, and meager industry. It still teemed with the destitute, the unemployed, and the down-at-heel. It still reeked of fish shops, hop yards, and unwashed humanity. And yet, there was no shortage of amusements, with a tavern seemingly on every corner, music halls like the Canterbury, Old Vic, and Gatti's, and plenty of entertainments of the flesh. This, of course, is what Dr. Thomas Neill Cream was most interested in.

The first unfortunate to encounter him was a pretty 19-year-old prostitute named Ellen "Nellie" Donworth. Nellie shared a room near Commercial Street with an army private named Ernest Linnell, who didn't seem to mind her occupation. At around six o'clock on the evening of October 13, she left her abode after telling a friend, Annie Clements, that she was going to meet a gentleman.

Later that evening, another friend, Constance Linfield, saw Nellie walking arm in arm with a "topper," (Victorian slang for a well-dressed gentleman in a top hat). Not long after, James Styles spotted Nellie alone, leaning on a gate on Morpeth Place. She was barely able to stand and Styles, at first, assumed that she was drunk. However, as he got closer, he saw that she was in severe pain. He helped her back to her lodging house and put her to bed, but by this time she was convulsing and grabbing her abdomen in agony. "That gentleman with the top hat gave me a drink out of a bottle with white stuff in it!" she moaned.

While Nellie's landlady remained with her, Styles ran to fetch an intern named Johnson from the nearby Lambeth Medical Institute. By the time they returned, Nellie's spasms were so severe that all of them together could not hold her down. The medic recognized her symptoms immediately as poisoning and instructed Styles to fetch a police officer. Nellie was then transported to St. Thomas' Hospital. She died before she got there.

A postmortem two days later found lethal doses of strychnine in Nellie Donworth's stomach. Coroner Thomas Herbert reported that the last several hours of her life must have been spent in extreme agony. Strychnine poisoning is a terrible way to die, characterized by extreme muscle convulsions and the feeling of being suffocated. In the final stages, the face turns blue and all of the muscles go rigid. Eventually the lungs contract to such an extent that the person dies from lack of oxygen, the face fixed in a macabre grin. Death can take anything from one to three hours. The person remains lucid throughout.

Cream bought his supplies of strychnine from Priest's Chemists, 22 Parliament Street. Because he was a certified doctor, he had no trouble getting what he wanted, although, by law, he was required to sign the poisons register. By following the entries in this journal, the police were later able to trace each of his deadly purchases.

Nellie Donworth had been given the poison in liquid form. For his next victim, Cream purchased a supply of gelatin capsules.

Twenty-seven-year-old Matilda Clover lived at 27 Lambeth Road with her two-year-old son, her landlord Mr. Vowles and his wife, and a servant girl, Lucy Rose. Matilda had turned to prostitution after her boy's father had deserted them. She also had an alcohol problem but had recently started visiting a doctor to cure that affliction.

On the night of October 20, Matilda left her room just after dark. Lucy saw her leave and presumed she was on her way to meet a man named Fred. Lucy only knew about Fred because she'd seen a note from him on Matilda's bedside table, asking her to meet him at the Canterbury.

At around 9 p.m. Matilda returned home in the company of a gentleman. Lucy got a good look at the man and would later describe him as tall and well dressed, in a cape and top hat. After leaving the man alone in her room, Matilda went out to buy some ale. A short while later the man left – alone.

At around 3 a.m., the entire house was woken by horrendous screams from Matilda's quarters. Lucy rushed to Matilda's room and was met there by the Vowles. As they entered, they saw Matilda lying naked on the bed, her body racked by convulsions. Contorted in pain, the woman screamed that Fred had given her some pills that had poisoned her. Lucy ran for a doctor, but it was too late. Matilda Clover died in agony at approximately seven in the morning.

Despite learning of Matilda's deathbed accusation against the mysterious "Fred," the doctor decided that she'd died due to mixing alcohol with a sedative she'd been prescribed. He recorded the cause of death as, "primarily, delirium tremens; secondly, syncope." It would be six months before the police realized that Matilda Clover was the second victim of the so-called, "Lambeth Poisoner."

In November 1881, a month after he killed Matilda Clover, Cream got a telegram from his family asking him to come home for the final disbursement of his father's property. He sailed from

Liverpool aboard the SS Sernia on January 7, 1892, returning to Britain four months later. Not long after his return, Cream became engaged to the pretty and respectable Laura Sabbatini. But if the nefarious Dr. Cream was seriously thinking about settling down to matrimonial bliss, he had no plans just yet of giving up his nocturnal ramblings.

Roaming Piccadilly one day, he spotted an attractive young woman who he reckoned for a streetwalker. Approaching the woman, Cream introduced himself, told her he was a doctor from America and was currently practicing at St. Thomas' Hospital. He invited her to join him for dinner at the Palace Hotel and there learned that her name was Lou Harvey. Lou (real name Louise Harris) was a bright young woman and despite Cream's urbane manner, she was wary of him.

Nonetheless, when he invited her to meet him later for drinks and a show at the Oxford Music Hall, she agreed. They arranged to meet at 7:30 p.m. Before leaving, Cream told Lou that he'd bring her some pills that would bring some color to her cheeks.

Cream arrived for the rendezvous at the appointed time. He and Lou then walked from Charing Cross underground station to the Northumberland Public House. They had a glass of wine, before walking along the Embankment. There, Cream suddenly stopped and produced the two capsules he'd promised. Lou had already decided that she wasn't going to take them, but she pretended to put them in her mouth. Then, as Cream looked away, she tossed the capsules over the Embankment. Once he thought she'd taken the pills, Cream suddenly remembered a meeting at St. Thomas' Hospital and departed, giving the woman five shillings to go to the theater. He promised to meet her there at 11, but of course, he never showed.

On April 11, 1892, Cream met Alice Marsh, 21, and Emma Shrivell, 18, in St. George's Circus and arranged to go with the two prostitutes to their flat at 118 Stamford Street, Lambeth. There, the trio had a few drinks after which Cream promised to give them some pills that prevented venereal disease, every working girl's nightmare in an era when customers did not use condoms. Cream spent several hours with the women, leaving eventually at around 2 a.m. Outside, he encountered the local bobby, Officer Comley, and the two exchanged greetings before Cream disappeared into the night.

At around 2:30, Mrs. Charlotte Vogt, landlady at 118 Stamford, woke to the sound of screams. She quickly roused her husband and the pair hurried upstairs.

Alice Marsh lay in the hallway, her body wracked by spasms. From inside the room, Mr. Vogt heard a banging sound and found Emma Shrivell in similar agony, thrashing around, her body contorted into poses Mr. Vogt didn't think a human being was capable of, her foot slamming the wall as she fought for oxygen.

Vogt ran for a policeman, who, in turn, summoned an ambulance. But it was too late. The women were dead even before they reached St. Thomas'. An autopsy revealed deadly doses of strychnine, leading the police to link these deaths to that of Ellen Donworth, six months earlier.

The killer meanwhile, had concocted a plan whereby he might profit from his crimes. Money, of course, was not Thomas Neill Cream's primary motive. He enjoyed killing, of that there can be little doubt. However, he now initiated an ill-conceived blackmail scheme, directing extortion notices to a number of reputable London physicians, accusing them of committing the murders and offering to suppress the "evidence" he had – for a price. None of these eminent gentlemen took the bait and instead reported the extortion efforts to the police, something that would later come back to haunt Cream.

With the Metropolitan police having made the connection between the Donworth, Marsh, and Shrivell murders, they stepped up their hunt for the Lambeth Poisoner. Chemists' poisons registries were scoured for the names of known criminals, while the police hunted down and questioned any thug with a history of violence, especially violence towards women. When these efforts turned up no viable suspects they expanded their search beyond London. With the six-month gap between the murders (largely due to Cream's trip to Canada) the general belief among investigators was that the murderer was a maritime man who killed at his ports of call. This line of inquiry also led nowhere.

Like many serial killers, Dr. Cream's downfall was largely due to his own actions. He might have remained at liberty indefinitely, might even, like his hero Jack the Ripper, have escaped justice altogether. All he had to do was keep his mouth shut about the murders. But Cream couldn't keep his mouth shut, the world had to know of his genius.

In April 1892, a few days after the Stamford Street murders, Cream met a former New York City detective named John Haynes. The murders, having occurred just a few day's hence, were a hot topic of conversation and the two men got talking about them. Haynes was immediately impressed by Cream's knowledge on the subject, but somewhat confused when he mentioned two victims Haynes hadn't heard of - Matilda Clover and Lou Harvey.

After the two men had dinner together, Cream offered to walk Haynes through Lambeth and show him where the murders had been committed. The detective naturally agreed, but Cream showed him more than just the murder sites. Speaking in the third person, Cream related where he'd met each of his victims, where he'd taken them for drinks, where he'd passed his deadly prescriptions. It didn't take Harvey long to realize that what he was hearing was virtually a confession to the crimes.

The following day, Haynes took this information to his friend, Inspector Patrick McIntyre of Scotland Yard. McIntyre was intrigued by the story, in particular, Cream's mention of Matilda Clover. At this stage, Clover was still not considered a murder victim, but her name had been mentioned in one of the blackmail letters. As to the other name – Lou Harvey – McIntyre was as much in the dark as his friend. However, he made inquiries with the morgue, and when that turned up nothing, launched a search to find the woman.

Meanwhile, Cream was placed under surveillance while background checks were run which revealed his true identity (he'd introduced himself to Haynes as Dr. Neill). The police also learned that Cream had been convicted in America of murdering a man with strychnine. With this information in hand, McIntyre obtained an exhumation order for Matilda Clover. The subsequent autopsy turned up copious amounts of strychnine in her system.

The net that was closing around Cream drew ever closer when both Lucy Rose and PC Comley provided descriptions of the man they'd seen at the crime scenes. These closely matched Cream. And there was further evidence when a sample of Dr. Cream's handwriting was compared to the extortion letters and found to be a match.

Cream was arrested on June 3. The charge at this stage was not murder, but blackmail. However, the police wanted Cream off the streets while they built their murder case.

The inquest into Martha Clover's death began at Vestry Hall, Tooting on June 22. During the two-week hearing, a succession of witnesses stepped forward to build an ever-strengthening case against Cream. Still, the doctor seemed unfazed, even writing to his fiancé to tell her not to worry and to assure her that he'd been falsely accused and would soon be free.

Cream maintained his air of indifference throughout the first week of the proceedings and through most of the second. Then, on the penultimate day, a witness was introduced who caused his mask to slip. The police had finally succeeded in tracking down Lou Harvey. As she strode confidently forward, Cream did a double take, removed his spectacles, polished them, and then replaced them on his nose. It was as though he'd seen a ghost and to him, of course, Lou was a ghost. He was sure that he'd killed her.

Lou Harvey's testimony sealed Thomas Cream's fate. On July 13, the inquest concluded that Cream had administered strychnine to Matilda Clover, thereby causing her death. He was removed to Newgate Prison, to await trial for murder. In subsequent weeks, he was also charged with premeditated homicide in the deaths of Nellie Donworth, Alice Marsh, and Emma Shrivell. A charge of attempted murder was added for Lou Harvey, and there were also charges of blackmail to answer.

The trial of Dr. Thomas Neill Cream took place over a five-day period from October 17 to 21, Justice Henry Hawkins presiding. The prosecution produced pretty much the same line-up of witnesses they'd called at the inquest while the defense produced none, their strategy focused on discrediting the evidence as circumstantial. It was never likely to succeed. The jury took just 10 minutes of deliberation before pronouncing Cream guilty.

Cream went to the gallows on November 16, 1892. But he would not go quietly to his grave. In the moment just before the trapdoor was sprung, he shouted from under the hood, "I am Jack –". The rest of the phrase was extinguished as he plunged to his death. Over a century later, debate still rages as to what Cream meant to say, the consensus being that he intended identifying himself as Jack the Ripper.

On the face of it, Cream makes a compelling Ripper suspect. Quite clearly, he had a pathological hatred of women in general, and prostitutes in particular. He also had a medical background – something that most Ripper experts believe was true of Jack. And although he was slightly taller than the man spotted with some of the Ripper victims, he resembled him in other respects.

So, was Dr. Thomas Neill Cream the elusive Jack? Unfortunately for those who seek an answer to the mystery, he was not. The Ripper murders took place in 1888, at which time Cream was serving a life sentence at Joliet, on the other side of the Atlantic.

Beverley Allitt

Angel of Death

Medical practitioners, whether doctors or nurses, are placed in a unique position of trust. Quite literally, we trust them with our lives. But what if one of these individuals, for whatever reason, decides to do harm to those in their care? When this happens, the results can be catastrophic, as more than 200 victims of Dr. Harold Shipman found out to their cost. Beverley Allitt did not murder nearly as many as Shipman, but in many ways, her crimes are even more shocking. This is because Allitt targeted the most vulnerable victims of all. She killed babies.

How Allitt ever came to be a nurse is a stern indictment of the systems in place to filter out individuals like her. One of four children, she exhibited some worrying signs early on. As a child, she enjoyed wearing bandages and casts and drawing awareness to her numerous ailments as a way of getting attention. And as she grew into an overweight adolescent, the behavior became even more pronounced. She took to spending considerable time at hospitals for a whole series of afflictions - gall bladder and urinary infections, headaches, vomiting, blurred vision, appendicitis, back trouble, and ulcers, to name just a few. She even, at one stage, convinced a doctor to remove a perfectly healthy appendix. Then, once the operation was completed, she took to picking at the surgical scar, preventing it from healing. She also indulged in other forms of self-harm, injuring herself with a hammer and with shards of glass. When one doctor cottoned on to her game, she simply moved on to another and began the charade all over again.

There is, of course, a name for this condition. It's called Munchausen's Syndrome, but by the time Allitt signed up to train as a nurse, she had not yet been diagnosed with it.

Allitt was a poor trainee, with an exceptionally high number of sick days and dire results in both written and practical examinations. She also displayed some odd behavior at the nursing home where she trained. She was suspected, for example, of smearing feces on a wall, and putting it into a refrigerator for others to find. Her boyfriend at the time also describes troubling signs. He says she was aggressive, manipulative and deceptive. On several occasions she claimed (falsely) to be pregnant. She also insisted that she'd been raped.

Yet, despite all of these warning signs, despite her failure to complete her nursing examinations, Allitt gained a temporary six-month placement at Grantham and Kesteven Hospital in Lincolnshire. The hospital was chronically understaffed and the ward Allitt was assigned to – Children's Ward 4 – had only two trained nurses on the day shift and one for nights. This is perhaps why Allitt was able to commit four murders, and attempt nine more.

The first victim was seven-month-old Liam Taylor, admitted to Ward 4 with a chest infection on February 21, 1991. Allitt went out of her way to meet Liam's parents and assure them that he would get the best possible care. She urged them to go home and get some rest. When the Taylors returned, Allitt told them that Liam had taken a turn for the worse and had required emergency care. However, she assured the concerned parents, he had come through it and was on the mend. She even volunteered for extra night duty so that she could be on hand if he needed her. The Taylors thanked her and said that they would spend the night at the hospital as well.

Just before midnight, while Allitt was alone with Liam, his condition suddenly worsened dramatically. He turned deathly pale and red blotches appeared on his skin and he began to have trouble breathing. Allitt shouted for an emergency resuscitation team, but their efforts were in vain. The little boy went into cardiac arrest, which resulted in irreversible brain damage. He was being kept alive only by life support machines and, on medical advice, his distraught parents made the heart-wrenching decision to turn off the support systems. Liam's cause of death was recorded as heart failure.

Yet the other nurses on the ward were confused. Why hadn't the alarm sounded when Liam had first stopped breathing? Only one person knew the answer, and Allitt was never questioned about the incident.

On March 5, 1991, just two weeks after Liam's death, Timothy Hardwick was admitted to Ward 4. The 11-year-old boy had cerebral palsy and had suffered an epileptic fit. Allitt immediately took over his care, making a great show of her concern for the patient. However, she'd only been alone with Timothy for a few minutes when she raced out of the ward shouting that he'd gone into cardiac arrest. By the time the emergency resuscitation team arrived, Timothy had stopped breathing and was turning blue. Despite their desperate efforts, the team was unable to revive him. Epilepsy was officially recorded as the cause of death.

Five days later, one-year-old Kayley Desmond, who had been admitted to Ward 4 on March 3, went into cardiac arrest after being attended by Allitt. The little girl had been brought in with a chest infection but had appeared to be recovering well. Fortunately, the resuscitation team was able to revive her and she was transferred to another hospital in Nottingham, where she made a full recovery. The attending physicians at Nottingham did, however, discover an odd puncture mark under her armpit. This was attributed to an accidental injection and no further action was taken.

Perhaps frustrated by her latest victim's escape, Allitt stepped up her activities, attacking three children over the next four days.

Five-month-old Paul Crampton had been placed in Ward 4 on March 20, as a result of a minor bronchial infection. On the day Paul was due to be discharged, Allitt was again attending him alone, when she called out that he was suffering from insulin shock. The emergency team rushed to the scene and doctors fought desperately to save Paul's life. Three times he slipped into a near-coma and three times they were able to revive him. Yet the doctors were flummoxed as to why his blood sugar kept dropping. Eventually, they were able to stabilize the boy and he was sent by ambulance to a hospital in Nottingham. Allitt rode with him, and on arrival, his insulin levels were again found to be elevated. Happily, little Paul survived the attentions of the Angel of Death, but it was only by a whisker.

The following day, five-year-old Bradley Gibson, suffering from pneumonia, went into cardiac arrest but was saved by the emergency resuscitation team. Blood tests showed perplexingly high levels of insulin but the boy's condition was stabilized and he appeared to be recovering. Then, after a late night visit from Allitt, he suffered another heart attack. Bradley was transported to Nottingham, where he made a full recovery.

Amazingly, given the alarming increase in crisis situations since Allitt's arrival, no one seems to have asked any questions. She was left to continue her dirty work unchecked.

On March 22, Allitt again raised the alarm after two-year-old Yik Hung Chan turned blue and appeared to have difficulty breathing. The boy was resuscitated with oxygen but later suffered a relapse after being left alone with Allitt. He was then transferred to Nottingham, where he recovered fully. His symptoms were attributed to a fractured skull he'd suffered as the result of a fall.

Allitt next turned her attention to two-month-old twins, Katie and Becky Phillips. The girls had been born prematurely, but after an extended stay in the hospital had been sent home in good health.

Then Becky suffered a bout of gastroenteritis and was brought to
Ward 4 on April 1, 1991. Two days later, Allitt raised an alarm,
claiming that Becky appeared hypoglycemic and was cold to the
touch. However, the response team found nothing wrong with her
and she was discharged that evening.

During the night, Becky suffered convulsions and a doctor was
summoned, who diagnosed colic. Her parents kept her in their bed
for observation, but she died during the night. An autopsy was
unable to find a clear cause of death.

As a precautionary measure, Becky's surviving twin, Katie, was
admitted to Ward 4, where Allitt was again in attendance. It wasn't
long before a resuscitation team was rushing to the ward to revive
Katie. Although their efforts were successful, Katie suffered a
similar attack two days later. She was rushed to Nottingham, but
on arrival, it was found that she'd suffered irreversible brain
damage as a result of oxygen deprivation.

Yet Katie survived and her grateful mother, still devastated by the
loss of Becky, asked Allitt to be Katie's godmother. Allitt coyly
accepted, even though she was responsible for inflicting paralysis,
cerebral palsy, and sight and hearing damage on the baby.

Allitt must have thought by now that she was invincible, that she
could continue attacking children with impunity. Certainly, no one
at Grantham was raising any questions about the sudden spate of
deadly incidents in Ward 4. Unbeknownst to Allitt, suspicions
were being raised at the Nottingham hospital that many of the

young victims had been sent to. Still, it would take four more attacks, and another death, before Allitt was finally found out.

Fifteen-month-old Claire Peck was brought into Grantham on April 22, 1991. Claire was an asthmatic who required a breathing tube. The child had been in Allitt's care for only a few minutes when the emergency team had to be called in for the first time. They managed to revive her, but a short while later Clare suffered a second heart attack and died.

In the wake of Claire's death, Dr. Nelson Porter, a consultant at Grantham, initiated an inquiry. The high number of cardiac arrests on Ward 4, over the previous two months, alarmed him. Yet even now, Allitt seems to have escaped suspicion. The hospital believed that an airborne virus might be to blame, although tests turned up negative. Then the autopsy results from baby Claire revealed an inordinately high level of potassium in the blood, caused by the presence of Lignocaine. This drug is commonly used during cardiac arrest but should never be given to a baby. Belatedly, the hospital called the police.

Superintendant Stuart Clifton, the officer assigned to the investigation, looked at the other suspicious incidents over the previous two months and immediately suspected foul play. His suspicions were firmed up when it was revealed that all of the victims had unusually high doses of insulin or potassium in their blood streams. Further investigation revealed that the key to the insulin refrigerator had been reported missing – by Beverley Allitt. And a check on daily nursing logs turned up another curious detail. Several pages corresponding to the near-fatal attack on Paul Crampton were missing.

As the police checked and rechecked records, interviewed staff
and spoke to parents of the victims, a common denominator began
to emerge. In 25 separate suspicious incidents, involving 13
victims, and resulting in four deaths, the only constant was
Beverley Allitt.

Within three weeks of the police being notified, Allitt was arrested.
She remained calm under interrogation and steadfastly
maintained her innocence. However, a search of her home
revealed the missing pages from the nursing log, throwing such
assertions into question. Further investigation revealed a pattern
of behavior congruent with a very serious personality disorder.
Psychologists who examined Allitt believed that she exhibited
symptoms of both Munchausen's Syndrome, and Munchausen's
Syndrome by Proxy (MSbP). Munchausen's is characterized by
attempting to gain attention through illness, while MSbP involves
inflicting injury on others to gain attention for oneself. It is highly
unusual for an individual to present with both conditions.

In November 1991, Allitt was formally charged with four counts of
murder, eleven counts of attempted murder, and eleven counts of
causing grievous bodily harm. She eventually went on trial at
Nottingham Crown Court on February 15, 1993. In the intervening
period, she had developed anorexia nervosa, and lost over 60
pounds in weight.

The evidence against Allitt was overwhelming. Prosecutors were
able to show how she was present at every suspicious incident and
how such incidents stopped immediately after she was removed
from her post. They were able to show high readings of insulin and
potassium in each of the victims, as well as unexplained needle

puncture marks. Allitt was further accused of cutting off her victims' oxygen, either by smothering or by tampering with equipment. A psychologist explained Munchausen's syndrome and Munchausen's by Proxy syndrome and showed that Allitt demonstrated symptoms of both. Allitt provided ample proof of this herself. During a trial that lasted 2 months, she was in court only 16 days, being too "ill" to attend on the other days.

The trial eventually concluded on May 23, 1993, with a guilty verdict and a sentence of 13 life sentences, the harshest ever handed down to a female defendant in British history.

Allitt was incarcerated at Rampton Secure Hospital, a high-security facility in Nottingham that houses individuals detained under the Mental Health Act. But even here, she continued her attention seeking behavior, stabbing herself with paperclips, ingesting ground glass, and scalding herself with boiling water.

She subsequently admitted to three of the murders, as well as several of the assaults. It is extremely unlikely that she will ever be released.

Peter Bryan

"I ate his brain with butter. It was really nice." – Peter Bryan

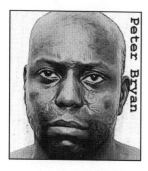

Peter Bryan should never have been allowed out of the hospital. Not with his history. Back in 1993, Bryan (then aged 23) had been working as a shop assistant in a boutique on the King's Road in London's fashionable Chelsea. There, he fell in love with a co-worker, 20-year-old Nisha Sheth, the beautiful daughter of the shop's owners. However, Nisha did not return his affections and Bryan decided to take revenge by stealing from the store. Caught attempting to smuggle out stolen items, he was fired from his job.

Given what we know about Bryan now, it is likely that he'd spent the days following his dismissal seething with anger at the perceived injustice. Then, on March 18, 1993, he was back, this time carrying a claw hammer. Nisha was talking on the phone when Bryan entered the store. Her 12-year-old brother, spotting the hammer in Bryan's hand, tried to intercept him. The powerfully built Bryan swatted the youngster aside then honed in on his target, raining down blow after blow on the helpless woman. By the time the ambulance arrived, Nisha Sheth was dead.

Bryan, meanwhile, had fled the scene. An hour after killing Nisha, he jumped from the third floor of a building in nearby Battersea in an apparent suicide attempt. He survived.

Diagnosed as a schizophrenic before his subsequent trial, Bryan pled guilty to a reduced charge of manslaughter, on the grounds of diminished responsibility. He was sentenced to an indefinite term at the Rampton maximum-security psychiatric unit. It was hoped that he'd remain there for a very long time.

However, just eight years later, psychiatrists recommended that Bryan be released to a residential care home. Then, early in 2004, the rehabilitation of Peter Bryan was complete when it was decided that he could come and go from the home as he wished. That fateful decision was made on February 17, 2004. That same evening, Bryan committed the murder that would gain him lasting infamy.

The victim was 43-year-old Brian Cherry, a friend of Bryan's who lived alone in a ground-floor unit in Walthamstow, east London. At around 7:15 p.m., Cherry's neighbor, and friend Nicola Newman noticed a strong smell of disinfectant from his apartment. Concerned, Nicola let herself in and was confronted almost immediately by Bryan as he emerged from the living room. He was bare-chested and was holding a large kitchen knife, which appeared to be bloodstained. The first words out of his mouth stunned Nicola. "Brian's dead," he said in a monotone.

At first, Nicola did not quite comprehend what Bryan had said. But as she looked past him into the living room, she saw Brian Cherry lying naked on the floor. It appeared that one of his arms had been separated from his body. Nicola backed out of the apartment and hurried to call the police.

Officers who responded to the call fully expected that Bryan would have fled by the time they arrived. He hadn't though. He was standing in the hallway, still bare-chested, still holding the knife, his hands bloodstained.

After taking Bryan into custody, the officers began a search of the apartment. One of the first things they noticed was a frying pan on the stove, a portion of what appeared to be brain matter congealing in butter. On the kitchen table was a plate containing another section of brain, a clump of hair attached, a trickle of pale blood oozing from the grey flesh. "I ate his brain with butter," Bryan later admitted. "It was really nice."

According to Bryan's version of events, he'd come to Peter Cherry's house with the express intention of killing and eating his friend. As soon as Cherry opened the door, Bryan attacked, bludgeoning the man into submission with his claw hammer. The pathologist would later count at least 24 blows from the hammer, delivered with such ferocity that Cherry's skull was smashed open.

Once Cherry was dead, Bryan used a hacksaw to saw off the top of his skull and gain access to the brain matter. He also started hacking off Cherry's right leg and both arms, using a Stanley knife. When this tool proved unequal to the task, he stomped on the corpse shattering the bone, then pulled the appendages free.

Bryan was sent to Pentonville jail, pending psychiatric evaluation to determine whether he was fit to stand trial. There, he told a staff member that he wanted to kill one of the guards and "eat his nose." On several occasions, prison officers had to use riot shields to remove him from his cell.

Transferred eventually to Broadmoor maximum-security hospital on April 15, 2004, Bryan was initially confined to his cell. But despite his violent history, he managed to manipulate the authorities into downgrading his security rating and moving him to a medium risk ward. It would have tragic consequences for another inmate.

Third victim, Richard Loudwell, was a murderer himself and was awaiting trial for killing an 82-year-old woman. At around 6 p.m. on April 25, 2004, Loudwell was in the dining room when staff heard three loud bangs. They raced over to find Loudwell lying on the floor. His face was covered in blood and there were signs of manual strangulation on his neck. Loudwell was rushed to the infirmary, but never regained consciousness and died just over a month later of the severe brain injuries he'd sustained.

His killer was not difficult to find and Peter Bryan readily admitted to the murder. "I wanted to kill him and eat him," he said, "But I didn't have much time. If I did I'd have tried to cook him and eat him."

Having twice failed in their duty to keep a dangerous psychopath off the street, the authorities eventually corrected their mistake by sentencing Peter Bryan to a whole life sentence, to be served at Broadmoor.

Bryan, meanwhile, holds out hope that he will one day be released, although he insists: "Cannibalism is normal. It's been here for centuries. If I was on the street I'd go for someone bigger, just for the challenge."

Peter Sutcliffe

The Yorkshire Ripper

"Apart from a terrorist outrage, it is difficult to conceive of circumstances in which one man could account for so many victims." – High Court Judge Mr. Justice Mitting

For just over 5 years, beginning in July 1975 and ending in January 1981, the women of northern England lived in terror of a vicious serial killer known as the Yorkshire Ripper. The fiend had a simple but brutally effective method, bludgeoning his victims with a hammer, before slashing and stabbing at their bodies with a knife and screwdriver.

Thirteen women would go to their graves at the hands of this evil man, seven more would survive but be left with severe physical, emotional and psychological scars.

Finally, after the most expensive manhunt in British history, an arrest for a minor misdemeanor ended the Ripper's bloody reign and put a name to the terrifying phantom. He was Peter Sutcliffe, a soft-spoken Yorkshireman, with a wife, a house, and a steady job. And as the police delved deeper into his activities they discovered a shocking truth. They'd encountered Sutcliffe before in the course of their enquiries, had, in fact, questioned him nine times, never once suspecting that he was the elusive Yorkshire Ripper.

Peter William Sutcliffe was born in Bingley, Yorkshire on June 2, 1946, the first son of John and Kathleen Sutcliffe. He was a frail baby, who grew to be a shy, introverted and puny boy. He had little interest in play and sports and preferred staying indoors and reading. This dismayed his somewhat macho father, and Peter found solace instead with his gentle, loving mother, Kathleen.

At school, Peter avoided other children and their rough-and-tumble games. This inevitably made him a target for bullies and led to him playing truant from school, which he'd always hated anyway. Later, he did try to fit in and much to his father's delight took up bodybuilding and developed an interest in cars. At the age of 15, with no clear focus or real prospects, he quit school and started work at the mill where his father was employed. This job lasted only a few weeks before Peter resigned, deciding it wasn't for him. Thereafter, he hopped from job to job, eventually ending up as a gravedigger at the Bingley Cemetery.

When Sutcliffe was twenty, he met Sonia Szurma, the daughter of Czech immigrants, now living in Bradford. Soon, he and Sonia were dating, although her parents did not initially approve of the union.

John and Kathleen Sutcliffe, though, were delighted, as Peter had never shown any interest in girls until he met Sonia.

In 1972, Peter's habitual tardiness eventually cost him his job at the cemetery. Thereafter he held a number of laboring positions before securing a job working the night shift at Anderton International. With a steady job now secured, and Sonia on her way to obtaining her teaching degree, the couple finally married on August 24, 1974, after an eight-year courtship.

On the surface, Sutcliffe was living an exemplary life, but some of those who knew him saw another side. Gary Jackson, who had worked as a gravedigger with Sutcliffe, would later describe how he'd steal the rings from corpses. Sutcliffe's brother-in-law, Robin Holland, said Peter would often brag about his exploits with prostitutes. Trevor Birdsall, who regularly drank with Sutcliffe, would eventually report to police his suspicions that Sutcliffe was the Yorkshire Ripper.

Birdsall described an incident in Bradford in 1969, when Sutcliffe claimed to have assaulted a prostitute by hitting her over the head with a stone in a sock.

Although stunned by the blow the woman was able to jot down the license plate of Birdsall's van. The following day, Sutcliffe had a visit from the police. He admitted the assault but said he'd only struck the woman with his hand. Because it was his first offense and the woman didn't want to take it further, he was let off with a warning.

Six months after his marriage to Sonia, Sutcliffe was offered a redundancy package by Anderton International. He took the £400 package and used it to get his license to drive heavy vehicles and also to buy himself a Ford Corsair – white with a black roof. During the following month, Sonia suffered the latest of a series of miscarriages and the couple was informed by doctors that she'd never be able to have the children they both so badly wanted.

Not long after that news, on July 4, 1975, Sutcliffe carried out his first recorded attack. The victim was Anna Patricia Rogulskyj, an attractive blonde in her early thirties. On the night of the attack, she'd had an argument with her boyfriend and gone out alone. Arriving home at 1:00 am, she found the lights out, so she started banging on the door. When this produced no result, she removed one of her shoes and broke a window.

As she knelt to put her shoe back on, she was struck from behind. Anna was knocked unconscious by the blow, but Sutcliffe hit her twice more before pocketing his hammer and withdrawing a knife. He lifted Anna's dress and pulled down her underwear, then inflicted a number of deep slashes across her stomach. The voice of a concerned neighbor interrupted Sutcliffe, but he spoke calmly to assure the man that everything was okay. He then straightened Anna's clothing and fled the area.

Anna was found a short while later and rushed to Leeds General Infirmary where doctors fought for 12 hours to save her life. Miraculously, she survived, but would be traumatized by the attack for the rest of her life.

On Friday, August 15, Sutcliffe drove with Trevor Birdsall to Halifax where they drank in a number of pubs. It was in one of these pubs that Peter first laid eyes on Olive Smelt.

Forty-six-year-old Olive was out drinking with friends and later got a lift as far as Boothtown Road, a short walk from her home. Sutcliffe had been driving behind and now pulled the car to the curb and got out, telling Birdsall to wait for him. He followed Olive as she took a shortcut through an alley and struck her twice on the head then slashed at her buttocks as she fell forward. Just as quickly, he broke off the attack and ran away, returning to the car where Birdsall waited. He'd been gone less than 10 minutes.

Olive crawled from the alley and her cries attracted neighbors who called an ambulance. She would spend 10 days in an infirmary and a lifetime suffering depression and memory loss.

Although there were startling similarities to the Rogulskyj and Smelt attacks, the police did not link them at the time. It would be three years before they could confirm that the attacker was the Yorkshire Ripper.

In September 1975, Sutcliffe eventually found work as a delivery driver for a tire company. Exactly one month later, he would succeed in murdering his first victim and his reign of terror would begin.

Wilma McCann was a 28-year-old mother of four who worked as a prostitute in the Chapeltown district of Leeds. Her body was found on the morning of October 30, 1975, lying face upwards on a sloping grass embankment of the Prince Phillip Playing Fields, just 100 yards from her home. She'd suffered two hammer blows to the head and 15 stab wounds to her neck, chest, and abdomen. Traces of semen were found on the back of her underwear.

On the night of her death, Wilma had left her four children in the care of her eldest daughter, 9-year-old Sonia, to go out drinking. She drank heavily at a pub until 10:30 pm then left to make her way home. At around 5:00 am, the following morning a neighbor found Wilma's two oldest daughters huddled together at the bus stop waiting their mother's return.

The McCann murder investigation was assigned to Detective Chief Superintendent Dennis Hoban. However, an extensive inquiry, involving 150 police officers and 11,000 interviews, failed to get the police any closer to her killer.

Sutcliffe claimed his next victim in January 1976, when he stabbed 42-year-old Emily Jackson to death in Leeds. Jackson lived with her husband and three children. The family was having financial problems at the time, forcing her to work as a prostitute to make ends meet. Emily and her husband Sydney would drive their van into Leeds where Sydney would wait for his wife in a pub while she entertained men in the van. On the night of Tuesday, January 20, 1976, they left their van in a car park and had a drink together before Emily left to look for clients. When she didn't return by closing time, Sydney assumed one of her clients had driven her home. But she wasn't there when he arrived and hadn't returned by daybreak.

Emily's mutilated body was found at 8:00 am the following morning, just 800 yards from the pub where her husband had been waiting. She was lying on her back with her legs apart. Her bra was pulled up, exposing her breasts. She'd been struck twice on the head with a hammer, then stabbed 51 times to the neck, chest, and abdomen with a sharpened Phillips screwdriver. The killer had also stomped on her right thigh, leaving the imprint of a size 7 or 8 Wellington boot.

On March 5, 1976, Sutcliffe was fired from his job with the tire company after he was caught stealing. He'd remain unemployed for several months before he found another driving job.

That same month, George Oldfield, Assistant Chief Constable of the West Yorkshire Police, received the first in a series of letters by a man claiming to be the Yorkshire Ripper. In it, the author claimed to have killed a woman named Joan Harrison but made no mention of the McCann or Jackson murders. It was dismissed as a hoax, one of the many received by the police and newspapers.

On May 9, 1976, a 20-year-old prostitute, named Marcella Claxton, was walking home from a party when a man stopped to pick her up. He drove her to a field, where he offered her £5 for sex. When Marcella agreed he told her to get out of the car and undress. She said that she first had to urinate, so she got out and went behind a tree. In the next moment the man was beside her and she felt a blow to her head. He struck her again and she fell on her side and lay there stunned and bleeding. She could see the dark-haired, bearded man standing nearby, masturbating as he watched her. When he was done, he shoved a £5 note into her hand, warned her not to go to the police and drove off.

Once he was gone, Marcella stumbled to a telephone box and called an ambulance. The wounds to her head required 52 stitches and a seven-day stay in the hospital. Five years after the attack, she would still suffer from depression, headaches, and dizzy spells.

The Yorkshire Ripper attacks were by now the main topic of conversation among prostitutes and patrons of the many pubs in the Leeds area. In an effort to protect themselves, the streetwalkers began working in pairs and making it clear to their clients that the details of their car registrations were being recorded. Police activity also increased in red-light areas and for a while, it seemed to be working – the Ripper was not heard from for another five months.

During the summer of 1976, Denis Hoban was promoted and Detective Chief Superintendent Jim Hobson became lead investigator on the Yorkshire Ripper case.

Peter Sutcliffe meanwhile, had some good news on the job front. In October 1976 he found work with T & WH Clark (Holdings Ltd) on the Canal Road Industrial Estate, between Shipley and Bradford.

On Saturday, February 5, 1977, 28-year-old Irene Richardson left her rooming house in Chapeltown to go to a nightclub. The following morning she was found lying face down in Soldier's Field (the same place where Sutcliffe had attacked Marcella Claxton). She had suffered three hammer blows to the head, resulting in a massive skull fracture. One of the blows had been delivered with such force that circular piece of bone had actually penetrated her brain. She had also been stabbed in the neck, throat and stomach, the latter wound so deep that her intestines had spilled out.

A tire mark found near the corpse was determined to be an "India Autoway" brand and with the help of tire manufacturers, a list of 26 car models was drawn up. It seemed a genuine clue but investigators hopes were soon extinguished when they learned that there were over 100,000 possible matches.

Patricia Atkinson operated as a prostitute out of her small apartment at number 9 Oak Avenue in Bradford and had often told friends she was safe from the Ripper because he killed outdoors.

On Saturday, April 23, Patricia was seen drinking in several pubs before heading home at around 11 p.m. On the way, she encountered Peter Sutcliffe and drove with him back to her flat. As Tina opened the front door, Sutcliffe struck the back of her head with a ball-peen hammer then hit her three more times as she lay unconscious. He then removed her coat, pulled down her jeans and lifted her bra, exposing her breasts. Then he stabbed her several times in the stomach with a chisel before fleeing the scene, leaving behind a bloody print from a size 7 Wellington boot.

As the Yorkshire Ripper's crimes continued to dominate the front pages of the newspapers, Sonia Sutcliffe qualified as a teacher and she and Peter began planning to buy their first house. Sonia had already identified her dream home at number 6 Garden Lane, Bradford. On Saturday, June 25, 1977, she persuaded Peter to view it with her.

That same night, 16-year-old Jayne MacDonald went out with some friends. They went dancing leaving the club early enough to catch the last bus. However, Jayne's friends wanted to get some takeaways and she went with them, resulting in her missing her ride. A friend, Mark Jones, said he would ask his sister to give Jayne a lift, but the sister wasn't home when they got there. They continued walking, eventually reaching the Florence Nightingale pub at around one thirty. Jayne said she could call a taxi from a call box outside the pub and assured Mark she'd be okay, so the couple separated. However, when Jayne placed the call to the cab company there was no reply. She started walking again, heading for a playground, where Peter Sutcliffe was lurking in the shadows.

Two children found Jayne's body at 9:45 am on Sunday June 26. She was near a wall inside the playground where Sutcliffe had dragged her. She was lying face down, her skirt disarranged, her white halter pulled up to expose her breasts. She'd been struck three times on the head with a hammer and then stabbed repeatedly in the chest.

Jayne's father, Wilfred, was destroyed by her murder and died two years later, having never come to terms with her brutal death.

Jayne MacDonald's murder catapulted the Yorkshire Ripper into the national media. Up until now, the victims had all been prostitutes and, reflective of public bias, the victims had not garnered much sympathy. But with the newspapers reporting the "slaughter of an innocent young victim" public ire and fear were engaged. It seemed any woman was now fair game for the Ripper. Leads poured in, while officers called on 679 homes in the vicinity of the attack, and took nearly 4000 statements. None of these enquiries pointed to Peter Sutcliffe.

Sutcliffe waited only two weeks after the Jayne MacDonald murder before striking again. On Saturday, July 9, he drove to the red-light Lumb Lane district of Bradford where he picked up Maureen Long at a taxi rank. He drove Maureen to Bowling Back Lane where he struck her with a hammer before launching a frenzied knife attack on her abdomen and back. The barking of a dog caused him to break off the assault and flee. His car was seen speeding away from the area by a security guard who reported it as a "Ford Cortina Mark II, white with a black roof."

The next morning, two women heard cries for help and found Maureen Long lying grievously injured on the ground. Somehow she had survived, but it would take hours of surgery and weeks of convalescence before she was off the danger list. Unfortunately, she couldn't remember much about the attack and the details she did recall were misleading.

The Ripper task force had meanwhile swelled to 304 officers, who between them collected 12,500 statements regarding the attack on Maureen Long. The possibility that the Ripper might be a taxi driver was explored and dozens of drivers were interviewed. One cabbie, in particular, drew suspicion. Terry Hawkshaw was unable to provide satisfactory alibis for the nights of the murders and fit the general description of the killer. He was placed under 24-hour surveillance and questioned several times. His house was searched and he was required to give hair and blood samples, before eventually being cleared.

The real killer meanwhile had just bought his first home and his wife had begun her first teaching position at Holmfield First School in Bradford. He'd also replaced his white Ford Corsair with a red one.

On Saturday, October 1, 1977, a week after he and Sonia had moved into 6 Garden Lane, Sutcliffe drove to Manchester where he picked up prostitute, Jean Jordan. She directed him to a vacant lot where they had sexual intercourse. Sutcliffe paid with a crisp, new £5 note, which Jean stuffed into a hidden compartment of her handbag. Sutcliffe then attacked her, striking her 13 times with the hammer before hiding her body in undergrowth and driving home.

The Sutcliffes were planning a house-warming party the following day, but as they waited on the arrival of their guests, Peter began worrying about the £5 he'd given Jean. As it was a brand new note, he thought the police might be able to trace it back to him. When the party was over, he offered to drive some of the guests home and used this as a pretext to return to the murder scene.

He found the body exactly as he had left it, but couldn't find the handbag. Eventually, frustrated at his futile search, he took his frustration out on the corpse, stabbing and slashing it over and over in the breasts, chest, stomach, and vagina. He even tried decapitating the body but was unable to do so with the tools he had. Eventually, he gave up and drove home.

It hadn't occurred to Jean's husband to report her missing. Although, the two of them still shared a home they lived separate lives and she often took off to visit family in Scotland without telling him. He assumed that's where she'd gone. It was only when he read a report of the discovery of a young woman's body that he contacted the police. The description matched Jean, but the face was so badly battered that she had to be identified by her fingerprints.

On Saturday 15 October, officers searching the murder scene found Jean Jordan's handbag and recovered the five-pound banknote with serial number AW51 121565. This was a promising clue, as the Bank of England was able to determine that the note was part of a consignment sent to the Shipley and Bingley branches of the Midland Bank, right in the heart of Yorkshire Ripper territory.

Narrowing this lead down further, it was established that the note had been part of a bundle of five hundred pounds that had been distributed to a number of firms in the Bradford and Shipley area. One of those firms was T & WH Clark, and Peter Sutcliffe was one of the almost 5000 men interviewed during this stage of the investigation. He gave the officers no reason to suspect him and his alibis for the times of the murders were corroborated by his wife.

But, even as the police were trying to find the elusive owner of the
£5 note, the Yorkshire Ripper struck again. This time though, his
victim would survive to provide a strong identification of him and
his vehicle. On December 14, Marilyn Moore was on her way home
from the Gaiety pub when she encountered a man leaning against
his car on Frankland Place. The driver was about 5-foot-6 tall with
dark, wavy hair and a beard. He was wearing a yellow shirt, a dark
blue zip-up jacket and blue jeans. He asked her if she was "doing
business" and they set a price before she went with him to a
vacant lot about a mile and a half away. The man said his name
was Dave, and suggested that they have sex in the back seat.
However, when Marilyn got out of the car she found that the back
door was locked. In the next moment, "Dave" came up behind her
and she felt a searing pain to her head as he struck her. She
screamed loudly and he hit her again as she fell to the floor and
again when she was on her knees. She felt she was blacking out but
then a dog started barking nearby and the man suddenly broke off
the attack, got into his car and raced off. Marilyn managed to get to
her feet and stumbled towards the road where a man and a
woman stopped and called an ambulance. She was rushed to Leeds
General Infirmary where an emergency operation saved her life.

The police were in no doubt that Marilyn Moore had been attacked
by the Yorkshire Ripper and tire tracks found at the scene
confirmed this. But even with the description Marilyn was able to
provide, their man remained at large.

By the end of January 1978, the police were beginning to believe
that the unsuccessful attack on Marilyn Moore had driven the
Ripper underground. Unbeknownst to them, he'd already killed
again, on the night of 21 January, but the severely mutilated corpse
of Yvonne Pearson would not be found until the end of March.

Helen and Rita Rytka were 18-year-old twins, working as prostitutes on the streets of Huddersfield. The pair had developed a system to ensure each other's safety, spending no more than twenty minutes with a client and always returning to the same place. If one arrived back before the other, they were to wait. The system had worked well for them until Helen broke it on the night of Tuesday, January 31, 1978.

On that snowy evening, Helen arrived back at the rendezvous point five minutes before her sister and, rather than wait, went with another client. That client was Peter Sutcliffe. After driving to a local timber yard, he told Helen to get into the back seat. As she was doing so, he swung at her with the hammer, and missed. Helen tried to scream, but the next blow found its mark, connecting with her head. She immediately collapsed to the ground. It was then that Sutcliffe realized they were in full view of two taxi drivers who stood talking nearby. He grabbed Helen by the hair and dragged her further into the wood yard, where he struck her again with the hammer. Then he lay on top of her, put his hand over her mouth, and raped her.

Finally, when the taxi drivers left, Sutcliffe got up to find his hammer, and Helen made a last desperate attempt to escape. Sutcliffe soon caught up with her, bludgeoned her into unconsciousness then stabbed her through the heart and lungs.

Rita had meanwhile arrived back at the rendezvous point and was concerned not to find her sister there. She waited for some time in the freezing cold, then decided that Helen had probably gone home without her. Fear of the police prevented her from reporting her sister's disappearance for two days. Helen's battered body was discovered by a police dog on Friday, February 3.

On March 10, 1978, the police received another letter from the man purporting to be the Yorkshire Ripper. The envelope was again postmarked Sunderland and the murder of Joan Harrison was again referenced. The author also threatened more murders, promising that the next victim would be old. The validity of the letter was called into question when the body of Yvonne Pearson was found on a strip of wasteland in Bradford on March 26, 1978. She'd been dead two months. If the letter writer was the Ripper, why hadn't he mentioned her?

The next Yorkshire Ripper victim was a 41-year-old prostitute named Vera Millward. On the evening of Tuesday, May 16, she'd gone the Manchester Royal Infirmary to pick up some painkillers. Her body was found the next morning, lying on its side in a well-lit parking lot. She'd been struck on the head three times, then slashed so brutally across the stomach that her intestines spilled out. Tire tracks were discovered at the scene. They matched those found at the other murder sites.

Eleven months passed before the next attack. During that time Peter Sutcliffe's beloved mother had died and he had gone into a period of deep mourning. In the intervening months, Sutcliffe had also been questioned again, after his license number that been noted in red-light areas. He explained that driving to and from work took him through those areas and the police left it at that.

On March 23, 1979, the task force received another letter, supposedly from the Yorkshire Ripper. The writer predicted that the next victim would be "an old slut" in Bradford or Liverpool. This prediction was to prove incorrect when the Ripper struck again on Wednesday, April 4, 1979. Josephine Whitaker, a building society clerk, was on her way home from a visit to her grandparent's home. It was only a ten-minute walk, and although her route passed an area of open grassland, the roads were well lit. Somewhere along the path, she encountered Peter Sutcliffe, who stopped her to ask for the time. As the young woman looked toward the town clock in the distance, Sutcliffe brought his hammer crashing down on her head. He struck her again as she lay on the grass, then dragged her away from the road and into the darkness. Alone with his victim, Sutcliffe unleashed a savage knife attack, inflicting 25 wounds to her breasts, stomach thighs, and vagina.

The next morning, a woman found Josephine's body and called the police. Soon after, Josephine's younger brother David set off for his paper round. As he approached the park, he saw police officers huddled around something lying on the ground. It soon became apparent what the men were looking at, and then David recognized his sister's shoe lying near the roadside. He ran home to call his mother.

The autopsy on Josephine's body produced an interesting clue, but unfortunately, one that would hamper the investigation. Traces of mineral oil were found on the body, and as similar samples had been found on the letters from Sunderland, the police began to consider that maybe the letters were genuine after all. On April 16, Assistant Chief Constable George Oldfield announced to the, now daily, press conference that they had an important breakthrough

in the case. A team of four detectives had been sent to Sunderland
to check on any engineering firms with employees who regularly
visited Yorkshire.

Two months later, Oldfield received a cassette tape from the
writer of the letters, who spoke with a distinct "Geordie" accent.
This tape was made public at the press conference of Tuesday,
June 26, resulting in 50,000 calls to the task force, already
overwhelmed by a sea of paperwork. In August, Stanley Ellis, a
Leeds University dialect expert, announced that the accent on the
tape was from the village in Castletown. This allowed the police to
further concentrate their efforts, but got them no closer to making
an arrest. On the contrary, the belief that the Yorkshire Ripper had
a Geordie accent was leading the police further away from the
Ripper.

On the evening of September 1, 1979, Barbara Janine Leach, a
student at Bradford University, went out for drinks with friends at
the Mannville Arms pub. Also in the pub that night was Peter
Sutcliffe. When the bar closed at 11:00 pm, he left. Barbara, along
with her friends, stayed to help the owner clean up and to have
another drink. When they left, at around 12:45am, Sutcliffe was
outside, waiting in his car. He watched the group walk towards
Great Horton Road where they turned left. However, Barbara
decided to go for a walk to clear her head. She asked her friend,
Paul Smith, to join her, but he declined. She then asked him to wait
up for her and left.

As Sutcliffe watched Barbara walk down Great Horton Road alone,
he started the car and drove past her then parked his car and got
out, armed with his hammer and knife. He waited in the shadows

until she passed then stepped out behind her and struck a single, fatal blow. He then dragged her lifeless body into the shadows and stabbed her eight times, before concealing the corpse under a piece of carpet and fleeing the scene.

Paul Smith waited for Barbara for over an hour, then went to bed. When she still hadn't returned the following morning, he called the police. A search turned up her body that afternoon.

The murder of Barbara Leach caused a renewed public outcry. It was all very well prostitutes being murdered in red light areas, but the last two victims had been "ordinary, decent women." The public demanded action and the police launched a massive £1 million publicity campaign involving newspaper advertising and billboards. Unfortunately, they still persisted with the misinformation that the killer spoke with a Geordie accent.

At the same time, the new Police National Computer was brought into the investigation. But while this innovation saved the police thousands of man-hours, it also created masses of new information that had to be checked. By the beginning of 1980, the police were swamped by millions of pieces of data, five million dealing with car registrations alone. They were quite simply unable to cope with the deluge.

Since January 1979, the police had returned many times to interview employees of firms like Clarks, where Peter Sutcliffe worked. In fact, Sutcliffe had been questioned so many times that his work colleagues began jokingly calling him "Ripper." And yet, despite matching the general description of the suspect, having his

Robert Keller

car spotted in red-light districts a number of times, having the right blood type and shoe size, and having possibly received the £5 note found in the possession of Jean Jordan, he was not considered a serious suspect.

In April 1980, Sutcliffe was in trouble with the police. Having been caught driving under the influence, he faced the very real prospect of losing his driver's license and with it his livelihood. A court date was set for January 1981. Before that date arrived, Sutcliffe would attack four more women, killing two of them.

The first of these attacks occurred in the respectable suburb of Farsley, Leeds on August 20, 1980. Marguerite Walls, a 47-year-old civil servant, had worked late that night to clear her desk before she went on holiday. She left her office building at 10:30 pm to begin the short walk home, her route taking her along well-lit streets. As she passed a house on New Street, Sutcliffe stepped from behind a fence and hit her on the head with his hammer. Stunned, but not felled, Marguerite started screaming, continuing even as he struck her again. He then grabbed her by the throat and strangled her as he dragged her into the darkness. Sutcliffe hadn't brought his knife with him this time. Instead, he pounded Marguerite's body with the hammer before concealing it under a pile of leaves in the driveway. She was found the next day, but because she'd been strangled, she was not initially considered a Yorkshire Ripper victim.

Sutcliffe next struck was in Headingley, home of the famous cricket ground. The victim was Dr. Upadhya Bandara, visiting Leeds from her native Singapore on a World Health Organization scholarship. On September 24, Dr. Bandara was walking home after visiting friends, when she was hurtled to the ground and struck with a hammer. However, before Sutcliffe could continue the attack, he heard footsteps and fled. Dr. Bandara's description of her attacker closely matched the man the police were seeking. Despite this, the police did not initially put it down as a Yorkshire Ripper attack.

On November 5, 1980, Theresa Sykes, a sixteen-year-old who lived with her boyfriend and their three-month-old son, was walking home from the Minstrel Pub in Huddersfield when she was attacked and struck three times. Fortunately, for Theresa, her boyfriend, Jimmy Furey, was standing at an upstairs window and witnessed the attack. He ran out of the house to help and Sutcliffe fled into the darkness. Theresa miraculously survived the attack, but she had to spend several weeks in the neurosurgical unit at Pinderfields Hospital, Wakefield.

On November 17, 1980, Sutcliffe was again in Headingley when he spotted Leeds University student, Jacqueline Hill, getting off a bus at the Arndale shopping center. Jacqueline had attended a seminar and was on her way back to her apartment at the Lupton Flats, where she had recently moved. She was only 100 yards from home when Peter Sutcliffe struck her on the head. Dragging her body to a vacant patch of land, screened by trees, he attacked her with a knife, stabbing and slashing. A worker at the Arndale center found Jacqueline's body the following morning.

The murder of Jacqueline Hill (wrongly believed to be the first Ripper murder in 14 months) unleashed a fresh outpouring of anger and a new deluge of information. The police received over 8000 letters, most of them anonymous. Most named suspects but only one named the real killer. Trevor Birdsall, Sutcliffe's one-time drinking buddy, had believed for some time that Peter might be the Yorkshire Ripper. Trevor waited for two weeks after sending his letter, and when the police had still not arrested Sutcliffe, he went personally to a Bradford police station and repeated his suspicions. Neither the letter nor his subsequent report elicited any police action.

However, luck was eventually about to run out for the Yorkshire Ripper. On Friday, January 2, 1981, Sutcliffe drove to Sheffield, a city where he had not killed before and one where potential victims were likely to be less vigilant. At around 9:00 pm, he tried to pick up a prostitute who declined his offer of £10. An hour later, another streetwalker, 24-year-old Olivia Rievers, agreed to go with him.

They drove a short distance to Melbourne Avenue and parked in the driveway of the British Iron and Steel Producers Association, where Olivia often brought her clients. As they sat in the car, Sgt. Robert Ring and Constable Robert Hydes drove along Melbourne Road as part of a routine patrol. They saw the parked car and had a good idea why it was there.

The officers pulled in behind Sutcliffe's Rover and questioned the couple. Sutcliffe gave his name as Peter Williams and said Olivia was his girlfriend, although when questioned he didn't know her name. Fortunately for Rievers, the officers knew her as a convicted prostitute and told her to get into the police car. Sutcliffe then said he needed desperately to relieve himself and the officers allowed him to do so in the darkness, next to an oil storage tank. Once out of view, Sutcliffe quickly removed and hid his hammer and knife.

The police had meanwhile called in the Rover's license plate number and finding it did not match the car, they took Sutcliffe into custody. He was driven to the police station in Hammerton Road, where he admitted that his name was really Peter William Sutcliffe. He said he'd lied because he didn't want his wife to find out that he had been with a prostitute. Sutcliffe was told that he'd have remain in custody for the night and be transferred to Dewsbury (where the false number plates had been stolen) in the morning. It was no more than a misdemeanor, but as Sutcliffe had been arrested with a prostitute, the arresting officers were required to call it in to the Yorkshire Ripper incident room.

The following morning, Sutcliffe was transferred to Dewsbury police station and the officers there noticed the number of similarities between him and what they knew of the Ripper suspect; his appearance, the fact that he was from Bradford where the murders had started; his shoe size, the fact that he'd been questioned by the task force on nine previous occasions.

Sgt. Ring meanwhile, had returned to duty at Hammerton Road police station and was told that Sutcliffe was still being held at Dewsbury station and was being questioned as a possible Yorkshire Ripper suspect. Ring then decided to play a hunch. Something had been bothering him about the trip that Sutcliffe had made into the darkness to relieve himself. Ring therefore returned to Melbourne Avenue to carry out a search. There, lying against a wall, he found the ball-peen hammer and knife that Sutcliffe had hidden the previous evening.

Things moved quickly after that. The police obtained a warrant and conducted a search of Sutcliffe's house, confiscating several items including a number of hammers. Sonia Sutcliffe was brought to Bradford Police Headquarters where she was questioned extensively for thirteen hours. And veteran Ripper investigator, Det. Sgt. Peter Smith was sent to Dewsbury to interrogate Sutcliffe.

Throughout the morning, Sutcliffe answered everything the investigators threw at him, but as the day wore on he began to lose the initial calmness he'd displayed.

At 2:40 pm, Detective Inspector John Boyle of the Ripper Squad told him that they'd found the hammer and knife. "I think you are in serious trouble." Boyle said.

Sutcliffe replied: "I think you have been leading up to it."

"Leading up to what?" Boyle asked.

"The Yorkshire Ripper," Sutcliffe said.

"What about the Yorkshire Ripper?" asked the detective.

"Well, it's me," Sutcliffe said.

Over the next twenty-six hours, Sutcliffe calmly related the details of his murderous career. The only time he showed any emotion was in describing the murder of his youngest victim, 16-year-old

Jayne MacDonald. The deadly reign of the Yorkshire Ripper was finally over.

Peter Sutcliffe went on trial on May 5, 1981. He entered not guilty pleas to the 13 counts of murder, claiming diminished responsibility. According to Sutcliffe he'd been instructed to kill prostitutes by a voice he'd heard coming from a gravestone in the cemetery where he'd worked. He believed it to be the voice of God.

The prosecution appeared willing to accept the plea after four different psychiatrists diagnosed Sutcliffe with paranoid schizophrenia. However, the trial judge, Justice Boreham, rejected the diminished responsibility plea. It would be up to the jury to decide on Sutcliffe's sanity and hence his responsibility for the crimes. Their verdict came on Friday, May 22, after a trial lasting 14 days. Sutcliffe was found guilty on all counts and sentenced to life imprisonment with the stipulation that he serve at least 30 years. This was later extended to a whole life term, meaning that Sutcliffe will never be free.

Five years of terror were at an end, but for the surviving victims, as well as the parents, relatives, friends and children of the deceased, a lifetime of pain and suffering still lay ahead.

Peter Sutcliffe, began his sentence at Parkhurst Prison but was later transferred to Broadmoor Hospital, under section 47 of the Mental Health Act of 1983. He has been attacked three times while incarcerated, suffering serious knife wounds and the loss of an eye.

Sonia Sutcliffe obtained a separation from Sutcliffe in 1982 and a divorce in April 1994.

The author of the Yorkshire Ripper letters, which had so hindered the police in their search for the killer, was finally arrested in October 2005. He was John Humble, an unemployed alcoholic who lived in Sunderland, a mile away from the village of Castletown. In March 2006, he received an eight-year prison sentence for perverting the course of justice. He is also a suspect in the Joan Harrison murder.

Kenneth Erskine

The Stockwell Strangler

"It tries to think for me. It says it will kill me if it can get me." – Kenneth Erskine tries to explain his murderous compulsion.

During the summer months of 1986, a brutal serial killer stalked the south London borough of Stockwell. The fiend, who became known in the media as the 'Stockwell Strangler,' targeted the elderly, entering their homes through unsecured windows. Once inside he strangled his victims to death before sodomizing their corpses and ransacking their apartments. In some cases he also performed a bizarre ritual, folding the victims' arms across their chests and tucking them up neatly in their beds as though they'd died in their sleep. Before the summer was out he'd have killed at least seven, and possibly as many as 11, victims.

The killer announced his presence on April 9, 1986, with the murder of retired schoolteacher, Eileen Emms. The 78-year-old was found dead in her basement flat at West Hill Rd, Wandsworth. She was lying in her bed, with no signs of a struggle and no obvious marks on her body, leading to the conclusion that she'd died of natural causes. However, after it was established that a portable TV was missing from the scene, the police were called in.

A post mortem revealed that Eileen had died due to asphyxiation caused by manual strangulation. There was also heavy bruising to her chest, which suggested that her killer had kneeled on her chest while throttling her.

Exactly two months later, on June 9, 1986, the police were called to the scene of another murder. The body of 67-year-old widow, Janet Cockett, was discovered in her flat on the Overton Estate in Stockwell, where she had been chairperson of the tenant's association. Mrs. Cockett had been the victim of a savage sexual assault, sustaining a number of fractured ribs as her killer kneeled on her chest and throttled her to death. There were a number of clues at the scene, some of them quite bizarre. For a start, all of Mrs. Cockett's family photographs had been turned outward, away from the death scene, as though the killer couldn't bear them looking at him. Then there was the nightdress, which had been ripped from the victim's body, but then neatly folded and placed on a bedside chair. In addition to these, the police were able to lift a clear palm print.

Another interesting clue came from the pathologist, Dr. Iain West. He established that the killer had strangled Mrs. Cockett one-handed, the other hand presumably placed over the victim's mouth to stop her crying out.

Although there were a number of startling similarities between the Emms and Cockett murders, the police at this stage were not connecting the two crimes. That view was soon to change.

In the early hours of June 27, 1986, retired engineer Fred Prentice was asleep in his room at a retirement home in Cedars Rd, Clapham, when he was awakened by a noise from the corridor. In the next moment, the door swung open and Mr. Prentice saw a young man silhouetted briefly by the light from outside. Then the man stepped into the room and closed the door behind him. Prentice barely had time to turn on the bedside light before the intruder jumped on the bed and pinned him down. He tried to cry out, but the man placed a finger to his lips and made a threatening gesture. He then began squeezed the old man's windpipe, relaxed his grip and then started squeezing again. While he was doing this, he kept uttering over and over. "Kill... Kill... Kill..." Prentice felt sure that he was going to die, but as the attacker relaxed his grip again, he rolled over and hit a panic button, triggering a silent alarm. The attacker then immediately released him and fled.

Fred Prentice had had an extremely lucky escape, but unfortunately, there would be no such luck for the next two victims. Valentine Gliem, 84, and 94-year-old Polish expatriate Zbigniew Stabrawa, lived next door to each other at Somerville Hastings House, an old people's home in Stockwell Park Crescent. On the night of June 28, 1986, just 24 hours after the attack on Fred Prentice, security staff at the retirement home noticed a young man loitering in the area. The man fled the scene as they approached him but, believing that he might have been trying to break in, the staff conducted an inspection of the building. It was then that they discovered the bodies of Gliem and Stabrawa. Both men had been manually strangled and sexually assaulted.

With these latest murders, the police had no doubt that they were hunting a serial killer. Detective Chief Superintendent Ken Thompson, a 45-year-old Scot with 26 years experience in the Metropolitan Police, was put in charge of the case. Thompson was allocated a team of over 350 officers, including 150 detectives. He immediately posted dozens of plainclothes officers to stake out retirement homes in the area.

It did no good. Two weeks after the horrific double murder, the Strangler struck again expanding his killing ground across the river Thames, to Islington, in north London. The victim was an 82-year-old widower named William Carmen, found dead in his flat on the Marques estate. The killer had tucked Mr. Carmen into bed, pulling the sheets up to his chin. He'd also ransacked the flat, taking £500 that the old man was known to keep in cash.

On July 20, 1986, the body of 74-year-old William Downes was found in his apartment on the Overton estate in Stockwell. He had been killed by manual strangulation, with no sign of forced entry into the premises. However, the police were able to lift an excellent new lead from the murder scene – a clear set of palm prints from the kitchen wall and another from a garden gate.

The investigators were by this time sure that the perpetrator was someone with a police record. Now all they had to do was to match the prints to their records. The problem was that, in 1986, Scotland Yard had just completed the mammoth task of transferring all of their fingerprint data onto computer. They hadn't even started on palm prints yet. This meant that the investigators had to match the prints manually and with a staggering four million files to work through, the task was nigh on impossible. Still, with lives at stake, it had to be done. The thing was to focus on the records most likely to produce a hit. They already knew that their perpetrator was adept at breaking in. They therefore focused their attention on London-based criminals with arrests for burglary. The search paid off three months later when they got a match to Kenneth Erskine, a small-time hood with a long arrest record for burglary and petty crimes.

The investigation team now had a name, but finding Erskine was not going to be easy as he was essentially homeless, a drifter and solvent abuser who lived in any number of squats and shelters. Unfortunately, they were unable to find him before he killed again.

On July 23, 1986, 80-year-old Florence Tisdall had spent the day watching the wedding of the Duke and Duchess of York on television. Like many of her generation, Florence held a special reverence for the royal family and she'd even had her hair done for the occasion. The following morning she was discovered at her upmarket apartment at Ranelagh Gardens, close to Putney Bridge. She had been manually strangled and sexually assaulted, the killer breaking several of her ribs as he knelt on her chest.

With this latest murder, the police search for Erskine intensified, the officers acutely aware that he could strike again at any time. However, despite scouring hundreds of south London squats, hostels, and shelters, they were no closer to tracking down their quarry. Then, they got a valuable break in the case, when it was discovered that Erskine was claiming unemployment benefits from a dole office in Southwark, with his next payment due on July 28. Plain-clothes officers were immediately dispatched to stake out the building. Erskine was arrested as he stood in line. He surrendered without a fight.

The investigating officers were certain that they'd caught the elusive Stockwell Strangler, but if they were expecting co-operation from Erskine they were quickly disabused of that notion. It was soon clear that their prime suspect was not dealing from a full deck, and as investigators looked into his background they realized that Kenneth Erskine was a very unusual character indeed.

Born in Putney to an English mother and an Antiguan father, 24-year-old Erskine was found to have the mental age of an eleven-year-old. Neighbors of the family remembered him as a chubby kid who enjoyed reading the Bible. But, from an early age, Erskine was a problem child who ended up being educated at a series of schools for maladjusted children.

Erskine appeared to inhabit a fantasy world, in which his homicidal tendencies were apparent from a young age. He imagined himself as Lawrence of Arabia, attacking, tying up and torturing smaller, weaker children. On more than one occasion, Erskine tried to drown other kids at the local swimming pool, and might have succeeded had staff not intervened. Another time, he attacked a teacher, stabbing him in the hand with a pair of scissors. A psychiatric nurse who tried to examine him was taken hostage, a pair of scissors held to her throat.

As a teenager, Erskine twice tried to hang his younger brother, John. Then, as a 16-year-old, he discovered drugs. After he tried to give cannabis to his siblings it all became too much for his mother, Margaret. She asked him to leave. He'd never see his family again.

Erskine spent seven years drifting aimlessly around London, living mainly in squats in Brixton and Stockwell. During this time he survived by petty crime and became an accomplished burglar, preying mainly (and significantly) on the elderly.

Two years later he attacked a youth with whom he was having a homosexual affair, slashing and stabbing at the boy as he lay in bed. That earned him a spell in a Borstal where he shocked staff with his paintings of elderly people in bed, burned to death, or with daggers protruding from their bodies and blood spurting from their necks. It was a chilling preview of what was to come, and alarmed prison doctors asked the authorities not to set him free him. However, with no legal right to retain him, he was released, and four years later embarked on his killing spree.

It was clear that the investigators were going to learn very little by questioning Erskine. He spent the majority of his many hours of interrogation giggling, fidgeting, staring out of the window, and masturbating. Yet he was clearly no fool. The police found in his possession details of ten accounts with various banks and building societies. Into these, he'd stashed a significant amount of money,

£3000 during his killing spree alone, whilst still drawing unemployment benefits.

Erskine went on trial at the Old Bailey on January 12, 1988, charged with seven murders plus the attempted murder of Fred Prentice. He readily admitted to burgling the homes of the victims but claimed that someone else must have been following him while he carried out the robberies, then entered after he left and committed the murders. The jury of seven women and five men gave short shrift to this ludicrous defense, finding Erskine guilty of all the charges. He was jailed for seven life terms, with a minimum of 40 years to be served before he is considered for parole, still the harshest recommendation ever handed out by a British trial judge.

He was subsequently diagnosed with a mental disorder and moved to the maximum security Broadmoor Hospital, where one of his fellow inmates is the Yorkshire Ripper, Peter Sutcliffe.

On February 23, 1996, Eskine intervened to save Sutcliffe's life after he was attacked by another prisoner, Paul Wilson.

Archibald Hall

The Monster Butler

Ah, the butler, the quintessential British manservant, discreet and unobtrusive, friendly but not familiar, keenly anticipative of the needs of his employer, graceful and precise in the execution of his duty. At least that is true of the vast majority employed in that noble profession. It was not true of Archibald Thompson Hall.

Archibald Hall was born in Glasgow on June 17, 1924. From an early age, he was involved in petty crime, leading to him being sent down for his first prison term at age 17. It would be the first of many such terms during which time he realized that he was bi-sexual.

In 1953, after yet another spell inside, Hall decided it was time for a change of scenery. He moved to London, adopted the name Roy Fontaine, and was soon involved in the city's thriving gay scene.

He also continued his criminal career, leading eventually to his arrest in connection with a jewel theft.

Sent to Blundeston Prison, Suffolk, for a ten-year term, Hall escaped in 1964 but was recaptured in 1966, with a further five years added to his sentence. He was paroled in 1972, but his liberty was short-lived. By 1973, he was back inside, remaining there until 1977. This time, though, he had put the prison term to good use.

Hall had always been the consummate actor, adept at playing an aristocrat or a wealthy American to pull off his various scams. Now he set about creating a new persona for himself, eradicating all traces of his Glaswegian accent, studying up on social etiquette and becoming a self-taught authority on antiques.

By the time of his release, he'd decided that he wanted to go straight and to this extent found a position as a butler in the household of Lady Hudson, the widow of an MP, near Waterbeck in Dumfriesshire.

To Hall's surprise, he found that he liked both his new job and his employer. However, he was in for a shock when Lady Hudson employed a new gamekeeper and gardener. He was David Wright, a former cellmate and lover of Hall.

Matters came to a head when Wright started pilfering the household silver and also threatening to reveal Hall's criminal past to their employer. Afraid that he'd be exposed, Hall struck on a plan to deal with the problem. He invited Wright to go rabbit hunting with him. Then, once the two men were in the woods, he shot Wright in the head, killing him instantly. Wright was confined to a shallow grave near a stream. A few days later, Hall resigned his position, much to the disappointment of Lady Hudson.

Hall returned to London in November 1977 and soon found a position with 82-year-old Walter Travers Scott-Elliott and his 60-year-old wife, Dorothy. He also hooked up with a former lover, Mary Coggle, and managed to get her a job as a maid in the same household. A short while later, Mary introduced him to Michael Kitto, a petty criminal and ex-con.

Hall had by now given up any pretense of going straight. The Scott-Elliot home was stocked to the brim with priceless antiques and other valuables. He figured he could pull off one big score and then retire. Michael Kitto was roped in to help.

On the evening of December 8, 1977, Hall along with Kitto and Coggle were casing the Scott-Elliott mansion. Mrs. Scott-Elliot was spending a few days at a nursing home and, while her husband was in the house, he was sleeping, under heavy sedation with the pills he was taking.

Believing that he had the run of the house, Hall gave his two accomplices the grand tour, pointing out particularly valuable pieces they might pilfer.   Unbeknownst to Hall, Mrs. Scott-Elliott had returned home earlier in the day and when he opened her bedroom door she demanded to know what he was doing and why he'd brought a stranger into her house.

It was Kitto who responded first, grabbing Mrs. Scott-Elliott to the throat and forcing her to the bed where, between him and Hall, they suffocated her with a pillow. Panicked now, with a dead body on their hands, the trio came up with a plan. They decided that if they could keep Mr. Scott-Elliott sedated, Mary could impersonate his wife for a few days. It would buy them some time while they decided on a long-term strategy.

The next day, they loaded the body into the trunk of the Scott-Elliotts' car. They then packed a confused Mr. Scott-Elliott into the vehicle, with Mary beside him dressed in his wife's furs and jewels. They drove to a cottage in Cumberland that Hall had rented, stopping on the way to bury Mrs. Scott-Elliott beside a lonely stretch of roadside near Loch Earn in Perthshire.

Having disposed of the body, the drove to the cottage. Leaving Mary with Mr. Scott-Elliott, Hall and Kitto then returned to London to ransack his home. They were back on December 14 when it was decided to murder the old man.

Kitto initially tried to strangle the 82-year-old, but he fought so fiercely that Hall weighed in with a spade and bludgeoned him to death. They then consigned him to a shallow grave in the woods near Tomich, Invernesshire.

Over the next day, the unholy trio bickered over how to split their loot. One particular bone of contention was Mrs. Scott-Elliot's mink coat. Coggle wanted to keep it; Hall insisted they should get rid of it as it was incriminating evidence. Eventually, the argument turned violent, with Hall bludgeoning Coggle with a poker and then suffocating her by placing a plastic bag over her head. Her body was disposed of in a stream as Hall and Kitto drove north to Glasgow.

After spending Christmas with Hall's family, Hall and Kitto returned to their hideout in Cumberland, this time with Hall's brother Donald in tow. Donald was a convicted pedophile and Archie had always despised him, so it didn't take much provocation to incite him to violence. After Donald began asking too many questions about his brother's newfound wealth, he was rendered unconscious with chloroform and drowned in the bath.

The next day, January 15, 1978, Hall and Kitto went looking for a place to dump the body. Unable to find a suitable spot, they left it in the trunk of the car and checked into the Blenheim House Hotel, North Berwick.

What Hall didn't know was that the police were already on his trail. An antiques dealer in Newcastle had reported that two men had tried to sell him silver at well below its market value. And the police had also found Mary Coggle's body and traced her as an employee of the Scott-Elliotts'. Calling on the Scott-Elliott home they'd found it in disarray, with bloodstains on the bedroom floor.

Now came the final twist that would land Hall and Kitto in custody. The hotel manager, aroused by their furtive behavior, called the police and asked them to check the registration of their vehicle. When the plates turned out to be false, the police arrived to question Hall and Kitto and turned up Donald Hall's body in the trunk of the car.

Hall soon broke down under questioning and confessed to all five murders. Convicted on four counts, both he and Kitto were sentenced to life imprisonment. Hall's sentence carried the stipulation that he would never be released.

Archibald Hall died of a stroke at Kingston Prison, Portsmouth, in 2002. He was 78 years old and was the oldest prisoner in Britain at the time.

Mary Ann Cotton

Serial Poisoner

Mary Ann Cotton (nee Robson) was born in the village of Low Moorsley, County Durham (now part of the city of Sunderland) in October 1832. Her parents were poor folk, her father a miner in nearby East Rainton. Like most lower class children of her era, Mary Ann had a harsh upbringing, her father's paltry wages barely enough to pay for the family's food and lodgings. Those who knew her spoke of her prettiness as a child and her beauty as a young woman. Perhaps this is true – she was certainly able to snare a succession of husbands and lovers – but the famous photograph of her, taken after her arrest, shows a rather plain, middle-aged woman.

Mary Ann's father was a strict Methodist who did not believe in sparing the rod on his children. He also insisted that Mary Ann and her younger brother, Robert, participate in various church activities. When Mary Ann was eight, the family moved to the nearby village of Murton, where she was enrolled at the local school. About a year after this move, Mary Ann's father was killed after falling 150 feet down a mine shaft at the Murton Colliery.

The death of the family's only breadwinner cast a dark shadow over the Robson family. There was a very real fear that they would be separated and end up on the streets or in the workhouse. However, this fate was averted when Mary Ann's mother, Margaret, remarried in 1843.

From the very beginning, Mary Ann had trouble getting on with her new stepfather, George Stott. He did not like Mary Ann, and the feeling was mutual. Still, she endured until the age of 16, when she left home to work as a servant in a wealthy household in South Hetton. Mary Ann was a hard worker but, by all accounts, also sexually precocious. Not long after her arrival, the village was awash with talk of her trysts with a local clergyman.

Ignoring the gossip, Mary Ann spent three years in service at South Hetton, before leaving to complete an apprenticeship as a dressmaker. In 1852, now aged 20, she married colliery laborer William Mowbray, by whom she had become pregnant. The couple moved to Plymouth, Devon, where over the next four years, Mary Ann gave birth to five children, four of whom died in infancy from gastric fever. Infant mortality rates were high in England at the time, but even by those standards, the Mowbrays appear to have been particularly unlucky parents.

And tragedy followed them on their return to the North East. Three more children were born, all of who succumbed to mysterious gastric ailments.

Perhaps because the marriage was so dogged by tragedy, it was not a happy one. The couple argued frequently, usually about Mary Ann's obsession with money. Eventually, the constant bickering got to William and he quit a very good job as a foreman at South Hetton Colliery to become a fireman on the steamer Newburn, out of Sunderland. This frequently took him away from home, leaving Mary Ann to care for the surviving children.

In January 1865, William suffered a workplace accident and returned home to nurse an injured foot. Mary Ann attended him during this time, although he had regular house calls from a doctor. Within weeks, he died suddenly of an intestinal disorder. William's life had been insured by the British and Prudential Insurance Co. Mary Ann profited to the extent of £35, equivalent to about half a year's wages for a manual laborer at the time.

Soon after William's death, Mary Ann moved her remaining children to Seaham Harbour, where she struck up a relationship with Joseph Nattrass. Nattrass was engaged to be married and after failing to break up the engagement, Mary Ann moved back to Sunderland. But not before burying her 3-year-old daughter, leaving her with only one living child out of the nine she had given birth to.

Back in Sunderland, Mary Ann found employment at The Sunderland Infirmary, House of Recovery for the Cure of

Contagious Fever, Dispensary and Humane Society, where she became a favorite with staff and patients alike due to her diligence and friendly nature. One patient, in particular, an engineer named George Ward, took a liking to Mary Ann. In August 1865, not long after his discharge from the Infirmary, Ward and Mary Ann were married at a church in Monkwearmouth. Mary Ann's surviving daughter, Isabella, meanwhile had been shipped off to live with her maternal grandmother.

George Ward had been in good health at the time of his discharge from the Infirmary. However, soon after marrying Mary Ann, he began to experience chronic stomach problems and to complain of paralysis in his limbs. Despite the diligent efforts of his doctors, he died in October 1866. Mary Ann again collected an insurance payout.

A month later, she showed up in Pallion and was hired as a housekeeper to shipwright James Robinson. Robinson's wife, Hannah, had recently died and part of Mary Ann's remit was to care for the children. Unsurprisingly, death soon visited the Robinson home, the baby of the family dying of a mysterious stomach ailment just before Christmas 1866. James Robinson, still grieving the loss of his wife, was distraught and Mary provided solace - and more. She was soon pregnant with Robinson's child.

In March 1867, just as she and James Robinson were discussing marriage plans, Mary Ann received word that her mother was ill. By the time she returned to her mother's home, though, the elderly woman was doing much better. Still, Mary Ann decided to stay awhile and nurse her mother back to health. Soon after, Margaret began complaining of new symptoms, unrelated to her original illness – she began experiencing severe stomach cramps. Nine days after Mary Ann's arrival, she was dead.

Mary Ann returned to the Robinson household, bringing with her, young Isabella (who had been living with her grandmother). Isabella arrived in perfect health, but soon developed an incapacitating stomach ailment, as did two of Robinson's children. By the end of April 1867, all three were dead.

With the death of two more of his children, James Robinson must have been wondering what he'd done to deserve so much heartbreak. Nonetheless, he appears not to have suspected any wrongdoing on Mary Ann's part. In early August, he put his mourning aside to wed Mary Ann at St Michael's, Bishopwearmouth. The couple's first child, Mary Isabella, was born in late November. By March 1868, she had succumbed to illness.

James Robinson meanwhile had become suspicious of his wife constantly pestering him to insure his life. Then he learned of debts of over £60 that Mary Ann had run up behind his back. He also found out that a number of household bills had gone unpaid, Mary Ann apparently pocketing the money he'd given her to settle them. The last straw came when his children told him that their stepmother had sent them to pawn various household items. Angered, he threw Mary Ann out. She left taking their young daughter with her. The child would later be returned to James Robinson after Mary Ann abandoned her with an acquaintance.

Mary Ann's worst nightmare had come true – she was penniless, homeless, living on the streets. Then, in early 1870, she met a friend, Margaret Cotton, whose brother, Frederick, had been recently widowed. Playing cupid, Margaret introduced Mary Ann to her brother. Within months, Margaret was dead of an undetermined stomach ailment and Mary Ann was left to console the grieving Frederick. Soon, she was pregnant with his child.

The couple was married in September 1870, at St Andrew's, Newcastle-upon- Tyne, Mary Ann not bothering to mention the fact that she was still legally married to James Robinson. She set up housekeeping in Cotton's house and quickly insured the lives of Frederick and his two sons, Frederick Jr. and Charles.

After giving birth to a son, Robert, in early 1871, Mary Ann learned that her former lover, Joseph Nattrass, was no longer married and was living in the nearby town of West Auckland. After rekindling the romance with Nattrass, she convinced Frederick to move the family there. By year's end, Frederick was dead of gastric fever and Joseph Nattrass and Mary Ann were living together. Mary Ann had, of course, also received another insurance payout.

At around this time, Mary Ann got a job as a nurse to John Quick-Manning, an excise officer who was recovering from smallpox. Following a now familiar pattern, she was soon pregnant by her employer. Marriage, however, was out of the question with three children and Joseph Nattrass still around, so Mary Ann got to work. Frederick Cotton Jr. died in March 1872 and the infant Robert soon followed. Then Nattrass became ill with gastric fever and died, but not before changing his will and leaving everything to Mary Ann. Now only Charles Cotton stood as an impediment to her plans.

In July 1872, Mary Ann asked a parish official, Thomas Riley, if Charles could be committed to the workhouse. Riley said that it would only be possible if she accompanied him, which she declined. She told Riley that the boy was sickly anyway and predicted that, "I won't be troubled long. He'll go like all the rest of the Cotton family." Riley was surprised by the comment as he'd met Charles and found the boy to be in perfectly good health.

Five days later, Riley was shocked to learn that Charles had died, apparently of gastric fever. He took his suspicions to the village police office and to the doctor charged with writing the death certificate. The doctor, who had attended to Charles recently, was also surprised by his death and, at Riley's request, delayed writing the death notice.

Mary Ann, meanwhile, was pressing the insurance company to pay out on the policy. On learning that payment was being delayed due to the death certificate, she called on the doctor and was startled to learn that there was to be a formal inquest into the boy's death. Mary Ann must have thought at this point that her luck had finally run out. However, the inquest seemed to vindicate her, finding no evidence that Charles had died by unnatural causes.

Charles was duly buried and Mary Ann collected her insurance payout and would likely have continued her murder for profit operation if the newspapers had not picked up the story. They reported on the inquest but also hinted that Mary Ann had been involved in a number of other mysterious deaths. Soon the small town of West Auckland was awash with rumor and suspicion and Mary Ann's latest paramour, John Quick-Manning, severed all connections with her.

With the whispering campaign well under way, Mary Ann began making preparations to leave town but was dissuaded from doing so by friends, who said it would look suspicious. Unbeknownst to her, moves were already afoot to prove her a murderess. A doctor who had participated in the inquest had retained samples of tissue from Charles Cotton's stomach. Now he tested those samples in his lab and found them to contain significant traces of arsenic. The doctor reported his findings to the authorities and, in short order, six exhumations had been ordered. All of the corpses tested positive for the presence of arsenic.

Mary Ann Cotton's trial began in March 1873, delayed by the birth of her daughter by John Quick-Manning. She was charged with a single murder, that of her stepson, Charles Cotton.

The case against her was damning with evidence of her purchases of arsenic, the long list of gastric fever victims in her past, and her statements to Thomas Riley about Charles' imminent death. Yet, Mary Ann steadfastly maintained her innocence, her defense claiming that Charles had died by inhaling arsenic used as a dye in the wallpaper of the Cotton home.

The jury was evidently unconvinced by this theory because they took just 90 minutes to find Mary Ann guilty of the murder of Charles Cotton. She was sentenced to death by hanging.

Mary Ann went to the gallows at Durham County Gaol on March 24, 1873. The executioner apparently misjudged the drop and instead of the instant death normally delivered by the noose, it took three agonizing minutes to send the heartless poisoner to her grave.

We will never know exactly how many she killed although estimates range from 15 to 21 victims, including; three husbands, ten children, five stepchildren, her mother, her friend Margaret Cotton, and her lover Joseph Nattrass. Her notoriety lives on to this day in a popular children's rhyme:

"Mary Ann Cotton --
She's dead and she's rotten!
She lies in her bed
With her eyes wide open.

Sing, sing!
Oh, what can I sing?
Mary Ann Cotton is tied up with string."

Where, where?
"Up in the air -- selling black puddings a penny a pair."

Dennis Nilsen

The Kindly Killer

"It was the beginning of the end of my life as I had known it. I had started down the avenue of death and possession."
– Dennis Nilsen

During the first week of February 1983, the residents of the small apartment building at 23 Cranley Gardens complained to their landlord that the toilets were not flushing properly. A plumber was called to investigate and said that there appeared to be a blockage in the drains that required a specialist. Two days later, a technician from a drain cleaning company arrived to take a look at the problem.

It was early evening when Michael Cattran lifted the manhole cover and descended into the darkness. He immediately picked up a peculiar smell, as though something had died down there. Then he noticed a thick sludge on the sewer floor and what looked like pieces of flesh. Startled by this discovery, Cattran climbed the ladder and placed a call to his supervisor. The supervisor told Cattran to close the drain and said he'd make an inspection himself the following day.

The next morning Cattran returned with his supervisor but noticed that the drain cover was in a different position. It was immediately clear why. It appeared someone had climbed into the drain during the night and cleaned out the suspicious chunks of flesh. But whoever had done it had been less than thorough. One piece remained, along with several small bones. The supervisor then called in the police.

Detective Chief Inspector Peter Jay was assigned to the case and arranged for the flesh and bones to be removed for analysis. By 3:30 that afternoon he had confirmation - the remains were human. He then returned to 23 Cranley Gardens, where he learned that one of the tenants, Dennis Nilsen, had been seen tampering with the drain cover during the hours of darkness. The detective went immediately to Nilsen's loft apartment. A knock brought the tall, bespectacled Nilsen to the door. Jay then informed him of the discovery of human flesh in the drains, at which Nilsen expressed surprise.

"Stop messing about," Jay told him. "Show us where the rest of the body is." Nilsen paused for only a moment before he spoke. "In two plastic bags in the wardrobe next door," he said. "I'll show you."

Later, with Nilsen under arrest and on his way to the police station, he was asked whether there was one body or two. "Fifteen or sixteen," was his reply, "since 1978."

Dennis Andrew Nilsen was born in Fraserburgh, Aberdeenshire on November 23, 1945. His father was a Norwegian soldier, Olav Magnus Nilsen, his mother, Betty Whyte, a native Scot. Olav Nilsen was a heavy drinker who showed little interest in his family, eventually deserting them when Dennis was 6-years-old old. By this time, Dennis was already living with his grandparents and had formed a very close attachment to his grandfather, Andrew Whyte. When Whyte died on Halloween 1951, the young boy was devastated.

In order to assuage Dennis' sadness, he was told that his grandfather was not dead but only sleeping. He was also allowed to see his grandfather lying in his coffin, which Nilsen later claimed was his most vivid childhood memory.

Despite his father's desertion and the trauma of his grandfather's death, Nilsen had a fairly ordinary childhood. He was a loner, prone to spending long hours walking the shore or staring out to sea. He had few friends, but developed a great affinity for animals. He remained sexually uninitiated at school, although he knew from an early age that he was attracted to other boys. Nilsen's academic record was unremarkable. He left school at 15 and opted to join the army.

The first three years in the army were the happiest of Nilsen's adult life. Stationed at Aldershot, in southern England, he enjoyed the discipline and hard work of military life and reveled in the sense of belonging, of no longer feeling like an outsider. Yet, there was an undercurrent to this comradeship, he felt intensely guilty about being sexually attracted to some of his comrades.

Nilsen's military posting was to the catering corps, where he specialized as a butcher (a skill he'd put to gruesome use in later years). He was popular with his colleagues, often joining them for drinks and taking his first steps towards becoming a heavy drinker.

He had his first homosexual encounter during this time, with a male prostitute while posted in Germany. And he developed a macabre fascination with death. He would whiten his body with talcum powder, blue his lips with food coloring and lay on his bed in a "death pose." Then he'd masturbate while looking at his "corpse-like" self in the mirror.

Although Nilsen enjoyed military life, and might have made a career of it, his growing political awareness began to sour him against the army. He became an outspoken critic of military intervention in Northern Ireland and eventually quit in 1972, having completed 11 years and 3 months of service.

In December 1972, he joined the Metropolitan Police, perhaps expecting to recapture the comradeship he had felt in the army. However, he found that police work was not to his liking and left after just one year. Thereafter, he struggled to make ends meet for a time before eventually finding work as a counselor at a job center. He'd remain employed there up until his arrest.

By 1974, Nilsen was living at 9 Manstone Road, North London and had become a regular at gay bars like the King William IV, the Colerne, The Golden Lion, The Black Cap, The Salisbury and The Cricklewood Arms. One night he met a man called David Gallichan and the two became involved in a relationship, eventually setting up house at 195 Melrose Avenue.

Nilsen and Gallichan spent two happy years together, but eventually the relationship waned and Gallichan moved out. Nilsen was left alone again. He consoled himself with heavy drinking and cruising the gay bars for casual sex partners.

As 1978 drew to a close, Nilsen was at an all-time low. Desperate for company on New Years Eve, he went to the Cricklewood Arms, where he met a 14-year-old youth named Stephen Dean Holmes. Holmes was on his way home from a rock concert and had only stepped into the pub to warm himself while he waited for his bus. However, he and Nilsen got talking and before long they were on their way back to 195 Melrose Avenue. Here they continued drinking, before crawling into bed together.

According to Nilsen's later confession, he woke up at around dawn, while Holmes was still asleep. He ran his hand over the boy's body and became aroused. However, he realized that his new friend was going to leave soon and he didn't want that to happen. Then he spotted his tie, lying on the floor where he'd discarded it the previous evening. He got out of bed to retrieve it, then slipped it around Stephen's neck, pulling it tight and simultaneously straddling the boy. Stephen woke and fought back, pulling then both to the floor but Nilsen held on, eventually strangling him into unconsciousness. He then filled a plastic bucket with water before lifting Stephen onto some chairs and allowing his head to drop back into the bucket.

"After a few minutes the bubbles stopped coming," Nilsen recalled. "I lifted him up and sat him on the armchair. The water was dripping from his short, brown curly hair."

Nilsen sat there shaking, barely able to believe what he had just done. He made himself a cup of coffee and smoked several cigarettes, trying to figure out what to do next. His small, black-and-white dog, Bleep, came in from the garden and sniffed at the corpse. Nilsen shooed him away, still uncertain what to do with the body. Eventually, he removed the tie from Stephen's neck and carried him to the bathroom. There, he gently lowered the body into the bath, ran some water, and washed the corpse's hair. After a time, he lifted the corpse from the tub and toweled it down. He then transferred the body to his bed and lay beside it, fondling the still-warm flesh.

Later that day, Nielsen bought an electric knife and a large pot. He intended dismembering the body, but when he got back to the flat he could not bring himself to do it. He found the corpse too beautiful. Instead, he dressed it in new underwear, then crept into bed beside it. He tried to have sex with the corpse but found he couldn't sustain an erection. Eventually, he fell asleep. Later he got up, made dinner and watched television with the body on the bed. Finally, he pried some floorboards loose and hid the body in the floor space.

After a week, Nilsen grew curious, so he lifted the carpet and removed the floorboards again. The corpse was dirty, so Nilsen carried it to the bathroom to wash it, climbing into the tub with it. Then he carried the body back to the living room. He was so aroused by the whole episode that he knelt down and masturbated into the corpse's stomach. Then he returned it to its makeshift grave under the boards where it remained for seven and a half months until Nilsen burned it in a bonfire in the garden. He added a tire to the fire to mask the stench of burning flesh. He raked the ashes into the ground.

In October 1979, nearly a year after the first murder, Nilsen met a young student from Hong Kong named Andrew Ho. He brought the man home, where he tried to strangle him. Ho managed to escape and reported the incident to the police, but no charges were brought.

Then, on December 3rd, 1979, Nilsen met Canadian tourist, Kenneth Ockendon, at a pub. They drank together for several hours and ended up back at Nilsen's flat. Nilsen said later that he had liked Ockendon and hadn't planned on killing him. However, the more time the spent together, the more desperate he became that Ockerdon was going to be flying home to Canada the next day.

Eventually, he strangled Ockendon with a cord from some headphones, washed the body and placed it in his bed. He spent the rest of the night with the corpse, fondling and caressing it. In the morning he pushed the body into a cupboard and went to work. Over the next days, Nilsen washed the corpse, dressed it and placed it in a chair beside him as he watched television. He also slept with it at night, pushing its legs together so that he could have sex between the thighs. Finally, Ockendon's corpse was placed beneath the floorboards, but Nilsen retrieved it several times, to sit with him as he watched television and to share his bed.

Five months later, on May 13, 1980, 16-year-old Martyn Duffey accepted Nilsen's invitation to spend the night. Nilsen strangled him into submission then drowned him in the kitchen sink. Later he washed the body and got into bed with it. Nilsen later said he kissed the corpse all over, then masturbated on its stomach. Duffrey was kept in a cupboard for two weeks before being placed under the floorboards.

The next victim was 27-year-old Billy Sutherland, a male prostitute. Nilsen barely remembers strangling him, saying only that he woke in the morning to find the man dead beside him.

Nilsen remembered very little about his next six victims, describing one of them as a "hippie-type," another as a skinhead and another an Irish laborer. He did remember his twelfth victim, though. Malcolm Barlow was a 24-year-old who suffered from epilepsy. Nilsen found him in a doorway near his home, having suffered an epileptic episode, and called an ambulance. When Barlow was released, he came back to Nilsen's house to thank him. Nilsen invited him in for a drink and killed him later that night. He now had half–a-dozen bodies hidden in various spaces in the small flat and although it was time to get rid of them he was reluctant to do so. He enjoyed having control over the bodies and most nights slept with one of them in his bed.

Eventually, after a neighbor mentioned the smell, Nilsen decided to dispose of the corpses. Stripping down to his underwear, he dissected them on the kitchen floor, calling on his butchering skills. He boiled the flesh from the heads using the pot he'd bought for that purpose. Then he packed the organs and body parts into plastic bags and stored them back under to floorboards until he could take them to the garden for burning. Some of the organs he threw over a fence to be consumed by rats and foxes.

It always amazed him that no one questioned him about his activities. At one stage neighborhood children came to watch the bonfire and he let them, warning them only to keep their distance to avoid being burned. On another, he spotted a complete skull amongst the ashes and crushed it before raking it into the earth with the rest of the remains. Nielsen would build three such bonfires at 195 Melrose Avenue, but soon he was going to be deprived of the use of his garden.

Nilsen had always been a combative person and had been engaged in a long-standing dispute with his landlord. The landlord had been trying to get him out for some time and an opportunity arose after Nilsen's apartment was burgled and trashed by vandals. Nilsen was offered a new apartment at Cranley Gardens and the landlord sweetened the deal by giving him £1000 to move out. Inexplicably, Nilsen agreed.

The apartment Nilsen moved to was one of six units at 23 Cranley Gardens. It was in the attic, so there were no floorboards to be lifted for the convenient storage of corpses. In addition, there was no garden for him to use. Perhaps, this is what Nilsen wanted. Perhaps he believed it would stop him killing again. It didn't.

Just six months after moving to Cranley Gardens, Nilsen brought a petty criminal named John Howlett home from a pub. After a few drinks Howlett climbed into Nilsen's bed. Nilsen told him to leave, but he refused. Nilsen then took a length of upholstery strap and started strangling the man. Howlett put up a fierce fight for his life and, at one point, Nilsen was certain he was going to be overpowered. However, he eventually got the upper hand and strangled the man into unconsciousness. He then dragged him to the bathroom and drowned him in the tub. Then he put the body into a closet and tried to figure out how he was going to get rid of it.

He decided to cut the body into small pieces and flush it down a toilet. He also boiled some of the flesh in his kitchen, along with the head, hands, and feet. The bones were separated and put into the trash, with some of the larger ones tossed over the back fence into a waste area. Other bones were sprinkled with salt and stored in a tea chest.

The second Cranley Gardens victim was Archibald Graham Allan, who was strangled to death as he ate an omelet that Nilsen had prepared for him. Allan's body was left in the bathtub for three days, before he was disposed of in the same way as John Howlett.

By now, Nilsen must have known that his method for disposing of bodies at Cranley Gardens was impractical, but it didn't stop him taking another victim. Steven Sinclair, aged 20, was a drug addict and petty criminal who Nilsen picked up in Leicester Square on January 23, 1983. Back at Nilsen's flat, they listened to music while Nilsen drank and Sinclair shot up. Soon after, Sinclair fell asleep and Nilsen strangled him with a piece of string. He'd later say that he felt he was doing Sinclair a favor by ending his suffering.

After Sinclair was dead, Nilsen bathed him and put him onto the bed. He then undressed and lay down next to the corpse. He'd placed two large mirrors beside the bed so that he could look at the two of them naked together. He kissed Stephen and talked to him as though he were still alive. Little did he know that the disposal of this corpse would prove his undoing.

The reason we know so much about the Nilsen case is because the man himself was so willing to talk about his crimes. Once he reached the police station, Nilsen quickly waived his rights and made a confession, describing each crime in sickening detail, speaking of his killing techniques, his methods of disposal, his macabre attraction to corpses. He showed no remorse and held nothing back. Afterward, he'd claim that it was his training as a soldier allowed him to remain so dispassionate, that deep down he was sickened and disturbed by what he had done.

A search of Nilsen's apartment, meanwhile, had uncovered several bags of dismembered human remains in various stages of decomposition. These were taken to a mortuary for examination. Nilsen himself directed the searchers to look in the tea chest and under a cabinet in the bathroom. He also accompanied the police to 195 Melrose Avenue and pointed out where he had buried and burnt body parts.

As the story broke, the police also heard from some of the victims who had been lucky enough to escape Nilsen's attentions. Douglas

Stewart described falling asleep in an armchair, and waking to find his feet tied and Nilsen putting a tie around his neck. He fought back, and managed to overpower Nilsen, and Nilsen then told him to leave. Douglas reported the matter to the police, who sent officers to 195 Melrose Place on August 11, 1980. However, after listening to Nilsen's side of the story, the officers decided that it was just a row between homosexual lovers.

On November 23, 1981, Nilsen's took a 19-year-old student named Paul Nobbs back home with him. The next morning, Nobbs woke with a terrible headache and went to the bathroom. In the mirror, he could see a deep red mark around his throat. His eyes were also severely bloodshot and his face bruised. Later that day, Nobbs visited the university infirmary and learned that someone had tried to strangle him. He decided not to report the incident.

In April 1982, Nilsen picked up a 21-year-old drag artist named Carl Stotter. After some time drinking together they went to bed. Stotter passed out but woke to find Nilsen throttling him. Nilsen then carried him into the bathroom and placed him in a tub of water, submerging him several times. When Stotter stopped struggling, Nilsen (presumably thinking he was dead) carried him to the couch. Nilsen's dog, Bleep, then jumped up and began to lick Stotter's face. The dog's show of affection probably saved Stotter's life. Nilsen thereafter carried him to the bed and held him until be regained consciousness. Later, Nilsen told Stotter that he'd gotten his throat caught in the zipper of the sleeping bag, and advised him to go to a doctor. A medical examination determined that someone had tried to strangle him. Despite this, Stotter did not go to the police.

Denis Nilsen's trial began on October 24, 1983, at the Old Bailey. He entered a plea of not guilty of murder, hoping instead to be found guilty of the lesser crime of manslaughter. In order for this strategy to succeed, the defense had to prove diminished responsibility, but they were unable to do so. Nilsen was found guilty of six murders and two attempted murders. He was sentenced to life in prison, with at least 25 years to be served before parole eligibility. The Home Secretary later imposed a whole life tariff, which means that Nilsen will never be released.

He is currently incarcerated at Full Sutton maximum-security prison in Yorkshire.

Michael Lupo

The Wolf Man

Michael Lupo was an enigma, the choir boy who went on to become a member of Italy's most elite commando unit; the special forces soldier who went on to become a hairdresser; the hairdresser who went on to become a serial killer.

Born in Italy, Lupo was raised in a strict Catholic family and served the church as both choir and altar boy. After school, the handsome young man joined the army and was accepted into an elite commando unit where he learned the techniques for killing with his bare hands. It was also while serving in the military that he realized he was gay.

You might think that a macho young man, serving in a Special Forces unit, would be confused by this realization. But not Michael. He fully embraced his sexuality, spending most of his free time in gay bars, aggressively pursuing sexual partners. Soon he'd discovered another quirk. He enjoyed sadomasochistic sex, with himself in the dominant role.

Lupo moved to London in 1975 and found work as a hairdresser, eventually saving up enough money to open his own boutique. The salon was almost instantly successful, attracting a wealthy clientele of gay men who were prepared to pay a premium for Michael's services. It afforded him an extravagant lifestyle, allowing him to buy a $300,000 home in Roland Gardens, South Kensington. But the other benefit of the boutique was equally important to Lupo, it was a magnet to scores of attractive young men, giving him a constant flow of new sexual partners. Lupo was outrageously promiscuous. He once bragged of having bedded over 4, 000 men.

Unfortunately, there is a price to be paid for living so carelessly, and it caught up with Michael Lupo in March 1986, when he was diagnosed with AIDS.

Lupo was outraged, infuriated and terrified by the diagnosis. He became surly, aggressive and uncommunicative, taking out his frustrations on those around him. He did not, however, curtail his sexual activities. Quite the contrary, in fact, he became more sexual aggressive. If he was going to die from AIDS he didn't see why others should be allowed to live.

But the knowledge that he was infecting his unsuspecting partners with a deadly disease was not enough to quell the rage living inside Michael Lupo. He required a more immediate outlet for his anger. He found it in murder.

On March 15, 1986, 37-year-old James Burns was out cruising the bars looking for a sexual partner for the night. Like Lupo, Burns had recently been diagnosed with AIDS, but that night he encountered something far more dangerous than the disease he was carrying. His body was found discarded in a basement the following day. He'd been strangled and mutilated with a razor, his tongue bitten off during the frenzied attack. He'd also been smeared with feces, something that would become Michael Lupo's calling card.

Three weeks later, on April 5, some children playing near a railway yard discovered the ravished corpse of Anthony Connolly. Police were called to the scene and found that Connolly had been strangled, slashed, and smeared with excrement. It was a near carbon copy of the Burns murder and clearly, the same person was responsible. An alarm went up. There was a serial killer on the streets of London, preying on gay men.

Lupo killed again on the night of April 18, although the murder was not linked to him until he confessed. Lupo had left a bar and gone for a walk to "clear his head." While crossing Hungerford Bridge, an elderly tramp approached him and asked for some change. The poor man got more than he bargained for. Lupo attacked him, beat him senseless and then strangled him to death and dumped his body in the Thames.

The following day, Lupo picked up a young man named Mark Leyland at Charing Cross Station and propositioned him to go into a public restroom for sex. Leyland initially agreed but then changed his mind, whereupon Lupo attacked him with an iron bar. Leyland managed to escape, but Lupo's next victim was not so lucky. Hospital worker, Damien McCluskey was last seen alive at a Kensington bar on April 24, 1986. His brutalized body, strangled, mutilated with a razor, and smeared with excrement, was found the next day.

On May 8, a young man walked into a London police station and reported an attack on his person. The man said that he'd met a stranger in a bar the previous evening and had agreed to go with him back to his apartment for sex. They'd left the bar together and the man had suggested they walk to the main road to hail a cab. However, the minute they were out of sight of the bar patrons, the man had looped a nylon stocking around his throat and tried to strangle him. Fortunately, he'd been able to break free and escape, but his neck still bore the ugly markings of ligature strangulation.

With three recent murders of gay men, and the gay community up in arms, the police were immediately alert. Two undercover officers were assigned to accompany the victim on a tour of various taverns in the hope that he might point out his assailant. On May 15, he pointed out Michael Lupo.

Lupo went on trial at the Old Bailey in July 1987. He entered guilty pleas to four counts of murder and two of attempted murder and was sentenced to four terms of life imprisonment.

Michael Lupo died in prison of AIDS-related illnesses in February 1995. He remains a suspect in the mutilation murders of gay men in Amsterdam, Berlin, Hamburg, Los Angeles and New York City. The murders all occurred while he was visiting those cities.

John George Haigh

The Acid Bath Murderer

"I have destroyed her with acid. How can you prove murder without a body?" – John George Haigh

On February 20, 1949, a man and a woman arrived at a police station in Chelsea to report that Mrs. Olive Durand-Deacon, aged 69, had disappeared. The woman was Mrs. Constance Lane, a friend of Mrs. Durand-Deacon, the man, John George Haigh, a fellow resident at the Onslow Court Hotel in South Kensington. Haigh told the police that the missing woman had made an appointment with him to visit his business premises in Sussex, but had failed to show. Mrs. Lane added that she'd first noticed Mrs. Durand-Deacon missing when she had not been at her usual seat for dinner the previous evening. When Mrs. Durand-Deacon also failed to appear for breakfast, Mrs. Lane had spoken to a chambermaid, who told her that the missing woman had been out all night and hadn't returned. She'd then decided to report the matter to the police and Haigh had offered to drive her.

The case was assigned to Sergeant Lambourne, who immediately set off for the hotel to query the staff and guests. In the course of these interviews, the officer grew suspicious of Heath. His answers seemed too slick, too contrived. And why was he, a middle-aged man, living in a residential hotel whose other residents were all wealthy older women? Lambourde decided to do a background check and soon turned up a lengthy rap sheet. Haigh had been arrested several times for fraud and had served three separate terms in prison for forgery, obtaining money by false pretenses, and theft. He definitely warranted further investigation.

The detectives' first port of call was Haigh's business premises in Crawley, West Sussex. Haigh had claimed to be a director of Hurstlea Products, but this proved to be a lie. He had, in fact, leased the two-story workshop from that company, to carry out what he called "experimental work." When the police searched the property they found tools, trays, and various chemicals. In addition, they found three carboys (narrow-necked, ten-gallon glass bottles used for storing acid). One of these was empty, another half empty.

The searchers also found a man's hatbox containing a .38 Enfield revolver that had recently been fired. Then there was a briefcase, monogrammed with the initials, J. G. H. This contained papers relating to a couple named Archibald and Rose Henderson, as well as a family named McSwan. There was a marriage certificate, several passports, identity cards, and driver's licenses. Soon an even more incriminating piece of evidence turned up, a dry cleaning receipt for a Persian lamb coat. Mrs. Durand-Deacon had been wearing such a coat when she'd gone missing.

The case against Haigh was strengthened further when a pawnbroker told the police that Haigh had brought in several pieces of jewelry on the day after Mrs. Durand-Deacon was reported missing. Haig had signed his name, "J. McLean" and given a fictitious address, but the pawnbroker knew him from previous business they'd transacted. The jewelry was recovered and identified by a relative as belonging to Mrs. Durand-Deacon. The police now had enough evidence to bring Haigh in for questioning.

Haigh seemed unconcerned about his arrest, reiterating his willingness to help investigators in their search for the missing woman. However, once the questioning got underway, he immediately began to lie about the evidence found at his workshop. He insisted that the coat had belonged to a Mrs. Henderson, and while he admitted that he had sold Mrs. Durand-Deacon's jewelry, he claimed that it had been to help the woman pay off a blackmailer. This was soon exposed as a lie, but Heath remained cocky, as though he were sure that the police couldn't touch him. Such was his arrogance that when left alone with a single detective, Inspector Webb, Haigh asked what the chances were of anyone being released from Broadmoor (an institution for the criminally insane). When Inspector Webb said nothing, Haigh decided to confess.

"If I told you the truth," he said, "you would not believe me; it sounds too fantastic for belief. Mrs. Durand-Deacon no longer exists. She has disappeared completely and no trace of her can ever be found again. I have destroyed her with acid." He then added proudly, "How can you prove murder without a body?"

At this point, Webb cautioned Haigh of his right to remain silent, but Haigh waved him away, clearly believing that he was above prosecution. This confidence, it would turn out, was based on Haigh's mistaken belief that the legal term 'corpus delecti' refers to the physical body when, in fact, it refers to the 'body of evidence.'

Over the next two and a half hours, Haigh gave a full confession to Durand-Deacon's murder. He had lured the woman to his workshop on the pretense of presenting her with a business opportunity, a process he'd discovered for manufacturing artificial fingernails. Once there, he'd shot her in the back of the head as she read some papers he'd arranged on a workbench. He'd then cut her throat with a penknife and drained some blood into a glass, which he'd drunk. Then he'd placed the body in a 45-gallon oil drum and dissolved it in sulfuric acid.

Before the officers even had a chance to absorb this bizarre confession Haigh was admitting to more murders. He'd killed five more, he said, draining a glass of blood from each victim before disposing of the bodies with acid. His motive, he said, was his need for blood, an obsession he'd had since childhood.

Haigh was remanded in custody, charged with the murder of Mrs. Durand-Deacon, and transported to Lewes prison, where he confessed to killing three more people for their blood - a woman from Hammersmith, a young boy from Kensington, and a girl from Eastbourne.

The police were unconvinced as to Haigh's supposed motive, seeing it as an obvious ploy to present an insanity defense at trial. However, with nine possible victims, the case was too big for the West Sussex police and they therefore requested a chief inspector and a pathologist from Scotland Yard. Chief-Inspector Mahon assumed charge of the case and went immediately to Haigh's workshop in Crawley to search for clues. As it turned out, there were plenty, including 28 pounds of human fat, three gallstones, part of a foot, eighteen bone fragments and a set of dentures. Haigh's hasty confession, delivered so superciliously, would ultimately prove his undoing.

John George Haigh was born in Stamford, Lincolnshire, on July 24, 1909, the only child of John Robert and Emily Haigh. His parents were members of the Plymouth Brethren, a strict religious sect who advocated an austere lifestyle, and limited interaction with the outside world. When Haigh was still a boy, the family relocated to the village of Outwood, Yorkshire, where his father constructed a 10-foot fence around their property to keep them separated from their neighbors.

Although he attended school, Haigh was not allowed to participate in sports or other extra-mural activities. To compensate, he developed an interest in music and became proficient at the piano and the organ, which he learned at home. Surprisingly, given their staunch anti-clerical beliefs, his family also allowed him to become a choirboy, meaning he had to attend Cathedral services in Wakefield. Haigh later said that he was confused by being allowed to participate in activities he'd been taught were sinful. He also said that the image of Christ, broken and bleeding on the cross, inspired his bloodlust. At around this time, he also claims to have been tormented by religious dreams involving a forest of crucifixes, all dripping blood.

After finishing school, Haigh took a job as an apprentice at a firm of motor engineers. However, his dislike of dirt soon outweighed his love of cars and he left after just a year. His next job was as a clerk with the Wakefield Education Community, but he soon quit that too, to take up a position as an insurance underwriter. Haigh enjoyed this work and did well at it. Yet, the lure of easy money, which was to prove his undoing later in life, derailed his promising career. He was accused of stealing a petty cash box and although no charges were pressed, he lost his job.

In 1934, Haigh married a 21-year-old woman named Beatrice Hammer but the marriage lasted only 4-months, ending when Haigh was arrested and subsequently sent to prison on a fraud charge. While he was incarcerated, Beatrice gave birth to a baby daughter, which she immediately put up for adoption. Haigh never saw his daughter and only once saw Beatrice after his release.

He was soon back at his old game. Typical of many serial killers, Haigh believed himself to be more intelligent than those around him. Prison had been a temporary setback, but he now believed he had a new scam that would net him a fortune. It involved selling cars that were still subject to a lease. He got away with this for only a few months before he was arrested and imprisoned for fifteen months.

While in prison, Haigh was excommunicated from the Plymouth Brethren, something which apparently disappointed him greatly.

After his release, he went into a dry-cleaning business, which initially did well, but failed after his business partner was killed in a motorcycle accident. Disillusioned by this failure, Haigh left his hometown for good and moved to London.

He hadn't been in the capital long when he became the chauffeur to a wealthy young man named William Donald McSwan. 'Mac,' as McSwan was called, owned a chain of amusement arcades and he and Haigh soon became firm friends. Haigh also got to know Mac's parents, who liked him right away and welcomed him into their home. As Haigh learned the amusement arcade business, Mac promoted him to manager. His prospects looked good. However, after just a year, Haigh announced that he was leaving. The McSwans were sorry to see him go, but, as entrepreneurs themselves, they understood his desire to go into business for himself.

The "business" that Haigh went into was yet another of his criminal scams. He set up a fake solicitor's office, then advertised an estate to be disposed of. Checks came in for the advertised property and Haigh cashed them, without supplying the goods. Like his other hair-brained schemes this one soon drew the attention of the police and he found himself back in prison, this time for four years. He'd barely been released when he was arrested for theft, resulting in a 21-month prison stint.

By this time it must have dawned on Haigh that he needed to try something different. Inmates incarcerated with him at the time would later recall him speaking at length about the money to be made from defrauding rich older women. He also became obsessed with the concept of 'corpus delicti' informing anyone who cared to listen that you could not be found guilty of murder if the police did not have a corpse. So often did he speak about this idea that he acquired the prison nickname, 'Ol' Corpus Delecti.'

It seems that Haigh had by now incorporated the idea of murder into his M.O. And he'd formulated an idea of how he meant to get rid of the bodies. Using sulfuric acid smuggled out of the prison's tin shop, he began experimenting on mice, noting the effects of acid on animal tissue. He believed he now had a foolproof way of disposing of incriminating evidence.

After Haigh was released from his latest stretch, he worked for a time for an engineering firm, and became engaged to the owner's daughter, Barbara Stephens, some twenty years his junior. Haigh was, of course, still married to his first wife, but he never bothered to inform Barbara of this inconvenient detail.

In 1944, Haigh was involved in a car accident and suffered a wound to his head. He would later claim that blood from the wound dripped into his mouth and reignited his bloodlust. While that is almost certainly untrue, 1944 was the year that he committed his first murder.

Haigh had, by now, moved to a basement apartment at 79 Gloucester Road. One night in August, he encountered his old friend 'Mac' McSwan, in a Kensington pub. Mac was delighted to see him and after a few drinks took Haigh back to see his parents. After that encounter, Haigh and McSwan resumed their friendship and for a time they were inseparable. Then, on September 9, 1944, McSwan disappeared, never to be seen again.

According to Haigh's later confession, he and McSwan were together at Haigh's apartment when he (Haigh) suddenly felt an overwhelming need for blood. Picking up a table leg he struck McSwan with it, knocking him unconscious. He then slit McSwan's throat, catching the blood in a mug before drinking it. He left the corpse where it lay, returning the following day with 40-gallon drum that he'd found on a bombsite. He then stuffed the body into the drum, and donning protective wear and goggles, began filling the receptacle with acid.

This proved more difficult than he'd anticipated and he had to take several breaks to escape the fumes. He also noticed that the acid became searing hot as it got to work breaking down the body tissue. Exhausted by his efforts, Haigh covered the drum and left, leaving his one-time friend to dissolve into a liquid sludge.

Haigh returned to the basement two days later. He looked into the drum and saw a black porridge-like substance, smeared with red streaks. The smell was horrific, but Haig used a wooden dowel to stir the mixture, to ensure that McSwan was fully dissolved. The liquid was thicker than he'd expected, but it was still sufficiently liquefied to allow him to pour it down a manhole. After completing that unpleasant task (made more so because of the chunks of semi-dissolved flesh at the bottom) Haigh cleaned up. Despite the difficulties, he was delighted with his first "experiment." There was no corpse for the police to find, no corpus delicti. Even if he was caught, he could not be tried for murder. Now it was time to claim Mac McSwan's property.

Haigh's first step was to visit McSwan's parents and tell them that their son had gone into hiding to avoid being drafted into the army. Mac had, in fact, voiced plans to do just that, so his parents had no problem believing the story. But in order to profit from his crime, Haigh now realized that he was going to have to get rid of the two older McSwan's as well. He began making plans to carry out their murders.

Haigh had learned a few lessons from his first "experiment" with acid. He knew that the fumes made breathing difficult, so he fashioned a mask to protect his face. He knew also that filling the drums with a bucket was impractical, so he acquired a stirrup-pump to transfer the acid from the carboy into the drum. Getting the body into the drum was also difficult, so he purchased an open steel tub and lined it with several layers of anti-corrosive paint.

On July 2, 1945, he invited the elder McSwans back to his workshop, bludgeoned them and then cut their throats. He then claims to have drunk their blood before dissolving them in the acid bath. He told their landlady that they'd gone to America, then took possession of their personal papers and began the process of transferring their property into his name. All in all, the triple murder netted him over £6000.

With his ill-gotten gains in hand, Haigh took a room at the Onslow Court Hotel, a residential hotel that housed mostly wealthy older widows. He gave his profession as a liaison officer between inventors and engineering firms and said that he had offices in several towns.

Haigh claims to have killed a young boy named Max in the autumn of 1945, but no crime matching his description was ever traced and the police believed the story was fabricated to support his insanity defense.

However, by 1947, Haigh was ready to kill again. It had been two years since the McSwan murders, and the money he'd leeched from their estates was all but used up. He needed to find a new source of income fast, and a chance soon presented itself.

Scouring the classified ads in the paper one day, Haigh spotted a house for sale. He contacted the advertiser, Dr. Archibald Henderson, and arranged a viewing. Haigh offered more for the house than Henderson was asking, but of course, he had no intention of buying the property. It wasn't long before he announced that he was regretfully unable to raise the money and the house sale fell through.

By that time he'd achieved his objective of involving himself in the lives of Henderson and his wife, Rose. For the next five months, he regularly saw the couple socially. Encouraging them to talk about themselves, he gleaned as many details as possible about their lives, families, and finances. Haigh had, by now, hired the workshop in Crawley and had moved all the tools of his macabre trade there.

In February 1948, Haigh visited the Hendersons and spent several days with them. Then, on February 12, he drove Dr. Henderson to Crawley on some pretext and shot him in the head with his own revolver, which Haigh had stolen. Leaving Henderson's body in a storeroom he returned to Mrs. Henderson and told her that her husband had fallen ill. Haigh then drove her to the workshop where she was similarly dispatched. The Hendersons were placed in acid baths and left to dissolve overnight. "From each of them," Haigh later said, "I took my draught of blood."

Haigh returned to the warehouse a couple of days later and threw the sludge into the corner of the yard, not even bothering to dispose of a foot that remained intact among the putrid mess. The following morning, he showed up at the hotel where the Henderson's had been staying. He settled their bill and produced a letter of authority from Dr. Henderson, empowering him to take their possessions and car. These he sold, along with the Henderson's house, realizing a sum of over £8000.

Unlike the McSwan's the Hendersons had relatives who were likely to ask questions. To circumvent this, Haigh wrote a series of letters, copying Rose's handwriting and forging her signature. He even managed to convince Rose's brother that the couple had immigrated to South Africa to avoid a scandal after Archie had performed an illegal abortion.

His next victim, according to Haigh, was a woman named Mary, from Eastbourne. Like the claimed murder of 'Max,' no evidence of this crime was ever found.

Haigh blew through the funds he'd stolen from the Hendersons in record time, due mainly to a gambling habit he'd picked up. By the end of the year, he was again broke, and with mounting debts. A number of attempts to lure people back to his factory failed, until

Mrs. Durand-Deacon accepted his invitation to view his process for manufacturing false fingernails.

But the murder of Durand-Deacon had netted him a pittance and there was no way for him to get his hands on her estate without arousing suspicion. He needed another wealthy victim, and fast. To make matters worse, he was contacted by Rose Henderson's brother, Arnold Burlin, who wanted to go to the police, and wanted Haigh to accompany him. Haigh agreed to the request and invited Burlin to journey to London and stay with him. It is highly likely that he intended murdering the man. Before that could happen, though, Haigh was arrested.

Haigh's trial began on July 18, 1949, at the Lewes Assizes. By now, the public interest in the case had been whipped into a frenzy by lurid tabloid headlines about the "Vampire Killer" and the small town of Lewes was overrun with visitors hoping to get a seat. The lines outside the court were long and most were turned away disappointed.

Haigh's defense team consisted of Maxwell Fyfe, G. R. F. Morris, and David Neve, their services funded by the News of the World newspaper, with whom Haig had promised to share his life story in exchange.

The prosecutor called on thirty-three witnesses, and rested his case on the afternoon of the first day. The defense, in contrast, called only a single witness -

Dr. Yellowlees, a psychiatrist who had examined Haigh and believed him to be insane. However, on cross-examination, Dr.

Yellowlees was forced into making a number of admissions that did as much good for the prosecution's case, as it did for the defense. Most pertinently, he admitted that Haigh seemed to know that he was doing wrong because he tried to cover up his crimes. With that admission, Haigh's defense lay in tatters. It took the jury only 15 minutes to decide that he was guilty.

John George Haigh went to the gallows at Wandsworth Prison on August 6, 1949. Prior to his death, he was fitted for a death mask by Madame Tussaud's for inclusion in its Chamber of Horrors. Haigh didn't mind at all. In fact, he bequeathed his clothing to the wax museum, on condition that they must always be kept in perfect condition. He seemed to enjoy his place in infamy.

Anthony Hardy

The Camden Ripper

On December 17, 2000, a man was walking along the River Thames near Church Road in Battersea, West London, when he noticed something in the water. As he drew closer, he was horrified to recognize it as the upper part of a woman's body, severed at the waist. The police were immediately called and the remains were retrieved from the river. Medical examiners later estimated that the victim had been in the water for a couple of weeks and had likely been cut with a large knife or a sword. They also noticed two distinguishing features; a tattoo of a rose on her upper arm, and a twisted lateral incisor tooth. These details were published in local newspapers in the hope of getting an identification.

It didn't take long before relatives came forward to identify the murdered woman. She was Zoe Louise Parker, a 24-year-old prostitute who worked the area around Feltham and Hounslow.

With that identity in hand, the police began making enquiries among the victim's known associates. However, with very little evidence to go on, they didn't hold out much hope of solving the case. Prostitute murders were always difficult to solve. They only hoped that this would prove an isolated incident.

Those hopes were dashed two months later with the discovery of another dismembered corpse. In late February 2001, three young boys fishing the Regents Canal at Camden retrieved a bag from the murky water. Upon opening it, the boys were horrified to find that it contained human body parts.

Again, the police rushed to the scene and when their initial search turned up nothing, divers were sent into the water. They retrieved another six bags, all of which contained body parts wrapped in garbage bags and weighed down with bricks.

The victim was later identified as 31-year-old Paula Fields, a Liverpool native who'd been in London for two years. Paula was a mother of two who worked as a prostitute to support her crack cocaine habit. She'd last been seen getting into a red car on December 13. The pathologist believed that a hacksaw was likely used to dismember the body.

As in the case of Zoe Parker, the time in the water had obliterated any physical evidence. However, in this instance, the police did have a viable suspect – Paula's ex-boyfriend, a local hoodlum with a history of violence. However, he was able to provide an alibi, and with no evidence linking him to the crime, investigators had to look elsewhere. The trail soon went cold.

Then, in December 2002, a series of horrific murders occurred in Camden, that bore many similarities to the Parker and Fields cases. Initially, the police did not believe that the crimes were linked. However, as their investigation progressed and they zeroed in on a particular suspect, they had cause to revise that belief. The suspect's name was Anthony John Hardy. His gruesome crimes would earn him the soubriquet, The Camden Ripper.

Anthony Hardy was born on May 31, 1951, in Burton-on-Trent, Staffordshire, the son of a coal miner. Unlike many serial killers who experience childhoods marred by physical and/or psychological abuse, Hardy's upbringing seems to have been happy and settled. In fact, the young Hardy was an achiever, with an exceptional drive to succeed. This coupled with a good intellect, allowed him to excel academically and he was ultimately accepted at London's Imperial College, where he gained a degree in mechanical engineering. He subsequently went on to manage a large engineering firm.

During the mid-1970s, Hardy reconnected with Judith Dwight, with whom he had attended university. The couple were soon married and moved to Tasmania, Australia, where they raised three sons and a daughter.

However, all was not right with the Hardy family. From around the early eighties, Anthony began to display the symptoms of mental illness. In 1982, he attacked his wife, bludgeoning her with a water bottle before trying to drown her in the bathtub. Charges were filed but later dropped when Hardy agreed to get psychiatric help and checked himself into a clinic in Queensland.

Following Hardy's release, he returned to England, where he and Judith were divorced in 1986, with her gaining custody of the children. Hardy appears not to have taken the divorce well. He began stalking his ex-wife forcing her to obtain a restraining order. However, this did little to discourage Hardy's attentions and he was briefly imprisoned after violating the restriction order.

Following his release from prison, Hardy again submitted to psychiatric care and was diagnosed with peripheral neuropathy, a disorder that is known to cause depression. He was also found to be suffering from bipolar disorder, for which he was prescribed medication.

No amount of medication, though, could put his shattered life back together, the one-time wealthy company director and devoted father, was a shambling mess. He spent most of the early-to-mid nineties as a homeless man, sleeping in various shelters and hostels around London. During this time he began abusing drugs and alcohol and picked up convictions for theft and being drunk and disorderly. He served six months of a one-year sentence in 1991 and was arrested again in 1998, after a prostitute accused him of raping her. The charges were later dropped for lack of evidence. Three further rape charges followed, similarly dismissed. As the decade drew to a close, Anthony Hardy was an ex-con, a homeless alcoholic, a diabetic, a mental patient who was ordered to seek psychiatric counseling.

Things began on a slightly better note in 2000, when Hardy was allocated a public housing flat on Royal College Street in Camden. The one-bedroom apartment was located a short distance from

Kings Cross, a locale frequented by prostitutes. This suited Hardy down to the ground, as he'd soon be trawling the area for potential victims.

In January 2002, a neighbor reported Hardy for vandalizing her home by pouring battery acid into her mailbox. The woman also told the responding officers that   something was amiss at Hardy's flat. There was a procession of women in and out of the apartment, she said, as well as bumps and thumps in the middle of the night, and what sounded like an electric drill being used at all hours.

The officers then conducted a search of Hardy's residence. Finding one of the bedrooms locked, they demanded a key, but Hardy said that he didn't have one. The officers then broke down the door and discovered the corpse of a young woman lying naked on a bed. Hardy was placed under arrest while a crime scene squad was called in and the body was removed to the morgue.

There was clear evidence of abuse on the corpse - cuts to her head, various bruises, as well as bite marks. However, just when investigators thought they might be dealing with a murder inquiry, the pathologist delivered a surprise. He said that the woman had died of a heart attack, not from foul play.

The deceased was identified as Sally Rose White, 38, a prostitute from the Kings Cross area, who was known to have an addiction to crack cocaine. White suffered from brain damage as the result of a birth defect and it was surmised that this, coupled with drug abuse, had caused a cardiac arrest. Her death was recorded as from natural causes. Hardy was free to go.

On December 30, 2002, a homeless man foraging through garbage bins behind a pub on Royal College Street made a horrific discovery. Inside one of the bags were human remains, including the severed sections of two legs. A police search of the garbage container, and others in the immediate vicinity, turned up eight more bags, stuffed with various body parts. Later, it was established that the body parts were from two women, although the heads and hands made missing, making identification difficult.

Crime scene officers meanwhile had picked up a promising clue. Spots of blood led from the dumpster back along Royal College Street. Following the trail, officers were led to a familiar location just a short distance away, a site where less than a year ago they'd recovered the corpse of Sally Rose White – Anthony Hardy's flat. Hardy, though, was nowhere to be found.

While a search was launched for the errant suspect, the police obtained a warrant and conducted a search of his ground floor apartment. They found a treasure trove of incriminating evidence - a hacksaw with human tissue still clinging to the blade; an electric power saw; various blood spatters; a woman's black stiletto shoe; various pornographic magazines; a pad with the notation "Sally White R.I.P"; and most damning of all, a woman's torso, wrapped in garbage bags.

Now the search for the fugitive intensified. It was suspected that Hardy may have left town, possibly even fled the country. However, on January 1, he was picked up on a surveillance camera at a London hospital. Hospital staff said he'd been trying to fill a prescription for diabetic medication and had waited four hours before leaving without his meds. He had smelled of alcohol and seemed very panicky.

On January 2, a sighting of Hardy was reported from the Great Ormond Street Hospital for Children in central London. Police quickly converged on the scene and arrested him. He put up no resistance as he was taken into custody.

Not long after Hardy's arrest, investigators were able to obtain the identification of the two victims whose remains had been discovered in the dumpster. Elizabeth Selina Valad, 29, was identified via a serial number on her breast implants, Brigitte MacClennan, 34 via a DNA match. Both were working prostitutes and known drug addicts. Both had had the misfortune of running into Anthony Hardy.

Anthony Hardy's murder trial began at The Old Bailey in November 2003. Hardy had initially been uncooperative with the police, but at the trial, he suddenly changed tack and pled guilty to the murders of Valad and MacClennan. Not only that, but he also confessed to killing, Sally White, the woman whose death had previously been ruled a heart attack.

During the trial Hardy revealed how he'd lured Valad and MacClennan to their deaths with promises of money and drugs. Once inside his apartment he'd engaged in "extreme sex" with them before strangling them and dismembering their bodies in the bathtub, using the hacksaw and power saw. He'd then packed up the remains and dropped them into the dumpster under cover of darkness. Sally White's corpse would have met a similar fate, he said, but the police had raided his flat before he'd had an opportunity to dismember her.

But that told only part of the story. In the run-up to the trial, investigators had been contacted by a friend of Hardy's, who handed over 44 macabre pornographic photographs that Hardy had sent him. The pictures were of Elizabeth Valad and Brigitte MacClennan and had quite clearly been taken post mortem. It was clear that Hardy was a pornography-obsessed necrophile and it was suggested that the motive for the murders was so that he could have access to the corpses to pose and photograph.

The trial concluded on November 25, 2003. Hardy was found guilty and sentenced to three life terms.

It has never been determined whether Hardy was responsible for the murders of Zoe Parker and Paula Fields. Any forensic evidence in those cases was destroyed by the time the bodies had spent in the water, and Hardy himself isn't speaking. However, the crimes certainly match Hardy's M.O. and the police believe there is a strong possibility he was the man responsible. He is also a strong suspect in at least five other murders in the Camden area during the time he was active.

Since Hardy's trial and incarceration, at least two other women have come forward to speak of Hardy's attempts to lure them into his apartment. Both resisted. Had they not they'd likely have ended up as victims of the Camden Ripper.

George Chapman

George Chapman was a rather unremarkable murderer, the serial poisoner of three women at the turn of the century. In fact, Chapman would have passed mostly unnoticed into the annals of criminal history, but for one startling fact. Some experts believe that he was Jack the Ripper.

Chapman was born Seweryn Antonowicz Klosowski, in the Polish village of Nargornak on December 14, 1865. Between 1880 and 1887 he trained as a surgeon in his native land before moving to London sometime in 1887. Because he had not completed his medical degree, Klosowski was unable to practice as a physician in England, so he found work as a barber, eventually running his own establishment in 1889. By then he'd adopted the English name, George Chapman. He'd also married a fellow Pole, Lucy Baderski (bigamously as it turned out, he already had a wife in Poland). In 1889, the couple moved to New Jersey, but Chapman was unable to settle and returned to England in 1892, leaving Lucy behind.

By 1895, he was living with a married woman named Isabella
Spink. Spink had a tidy sum put away in savings and in 1897,
Chapman convinced her to hand the money over to him, to invest
in a pub. A few months later, in December 1897, a doctor was
called to the establishment, where he found Isabella Spink stricken
with severe abdominal pains and vomiting. She died a short while
later, her death attributed to acute gastroenteritis. Chapman
inherited £500 from her estate.

In 1898, Chapman took one of his barmaids, Bessie Taylor, as his
mistress. The couple remained together for three years, until
1901, when another barmaid, Maud Marsh, caught Chapman's eye.
A short while later, Bessie Taylor came down with symptoms that
were startlingly similar to Isabella Spink. She died on February 14,
1901, leaving Chapman free to pursue his new love interest.

But his ardor for Maud Marsh lasted even shorter than that for
Bessie Taylor. Maud took to her sick bed in October 1902,
attended by her mother. By the 22nd of that month, she was dead.

This time, however, Chapman had miscalculated. Maud's mother
was certain that her daughter had been poisoned and insisted on a
post-mortem. The examination revealed copious amounts of
antimony in her system.

Chapman was placed under arrest, and an exhumation order was
issued for the bodies of Isabella Spink and Bessie Taylor. They too
were found to have been poisoned with antimony, a particularly
nasty substance, which produces symptoms similar to arsenic. The

source of the venom was soon revealed. Chapman had recently purchased tartar emetic from a local chemist.

With such damning evidence against him, it was always likely that Chapman would be found guilty. And so it proved. He was convicted at the Old Bailey on March 20, 1903. The sentence was death by hanging.

For a man who had no qualms about sending three innocent victims to an excruciatingly painful death, Chapman faced his own demise in a less than dignified fashion. On the day of his execution (April 7, 1903) he had to be carried to the gallows. Two burly prison guards were required to hold him upright as the trap was sprung.

But was George Chapman Jack the Ripper?

Frederick Abberline, the Scotland Yard detective who led the Ripper enquiry seems to have thought so. On Chapman's arrest, he supposedly told the policeman who brought Chapman in: "You've got Jack the Ripper at last!" Contemporary Ripper expert, Philip Sugden, tends to agree. He considers Chapman the most likely of all the named Ripper suspects.

Strengthening the case for Chapman as Jack are the facts that he arrived in Whitechapel shortly before the Ripper murders started, lived in the area for the duration, and left for America soon after they ended. He also trained as a surgeon, and the Ripper was believed to possess medical expertise. Additionally, while

Chapman was living in America, a New York woman named Carrie Brown fell prey to a Ripper-style killer.

But the case against Chapman is far from proven. Criminologists find it highly unlikely that a killer as vicious as Jack the Ripper would lay fallow for several years and then re-emerge to commit murder by the relatively "hands-off" method of poisoning. The Ripper also selected victims who were unknown to him, whereas Chapman killed his live-in lovers.

John Straffen

The Bath Strangler

"Is this about the girl I took to the pictures last night? When I left her she was dead." – John Straffen

John Thomas Straffen was born on February 27, 1930, at the Bordon military camp in Hampshire. His father, John Sr. was a professional soldier and John Jr. was the third of his children. When Straffen was two years of age, his father was posted to India, where the family spent six years. Returning to Britain in March 1938, Straffen's father received an honorable discharge from the Army and the family settled in Bath, Somerset. By that time Straffen had already proved to be a troubled child, while his older sister had been diagnosed with mental problems.

The Straffen family hadn't been back in England long when John was in trouble. In October 1938, he was referred to a Child Guidance Clinic for stealing and truancy. Then, in June 1939, he was hauled before a Juvenile Court for stealing a purse from a girl. That offense earned him two years probation, although his probation officer noted that Straffen had no concept of right and wrong, and did not understand what he had done to earn the probationary sentence. The official recommended that the boy should be assessed by a psychiatrist.

Straffen was found to have an IQ of 58 and a mental age of six. As a result, he was certified as mentally defective under the Mental Deficiency Act and sent to St Joseph's, a school for mentally challenged children, in Sambourne.

Two years later Straffen was moved to Besford Court, a senior school. Here, his caregivers recorded that he was a solitary boy who was rebellious and prone to violent outbursts. He seemed to push back against authority and took any form of correction badly. While Staffen was at Besford Hall, he was strongly suspected of strangling two prize geese, the property of one of the teachers at the school. However, there was no proof to definitely implicate him.

At the age of 16, Staffen underwent another series of competency tests and was found to have and IQ of 64 and a mental age of 9 years 6 months. This was deemed sufficient for him to be discharged.

Straffen returned to his family home to Bath in March 1946 where a Medical Health Officer examined him and found he still warranted certification under the Mental Deficiency Act. Despite this, he was able to find work, a number of short-term jobs eventually leading to employment as a machinist in a clothing factory. But his childhood preoccupation with burglary persisted. By 1947 he was regularly breaking into homes and stealing small items. Staffen didn't try to profit from these crimes, nor even give his booty away. He simply hid the stolen items in various caches. It appears the thrill he derived from breaking into homes was what he was really after.

On July 27, 1947, an incident occurred that provided a chilling foretaste of what was to come. After breaking into a house he thought to be empty, Straffen encountered a 13-year-old girl. Straffen grabbed the child by the throat, placed his hand over her mouth and whispered in her ear: "What would you do if I killed you? I have done it before."

This badly shaken girl reported the incident, but it was not connected to Straffen until weeks later. In September 1947, Straffen was arrested after strangling five chickens belonging to the father of a girl with whom he had quarreled. Under questioning, he cheerfully confessed to the crime as well as to a number of burglaries and incidents of vandalism of which he was suspected. He was remanded in custody and examined by the Medical Officer of Horfield prison, who found him to be mentally retarded. On October 10, Straffen was committed to Hortham Colony, a facility that specialized in rehabilitating mentally challenged offenders and helping them to resettle in the community.

Despite his threats of violence against the young girl, Straffen had only been charged with burglary and was therefore flagged as a non-violent offender. His file stated that he was "not of violent or dangerous propensities." He kept pretty much to himself at Hortham and his good behavior earned him a transfer to a low-security hostel at Winchester in July 1949. Staffen remained here for a year and was on his best behavior. However, after being found guilty of a petty theft, he was sent back to Hortham. In August 1950, he absconded from the facility and violently resisted the police officers sent to bring him back.

In 1951, Straffen underwent an electroencephalograph (ECG) at a Bristol hospital, which showed that he had suffered serious damage to the cerebral cortex, probably as a result of encephalitis he'd suffered in India at the age of six. He was still, though, considered non-violent and was allowed a period of unescorted home leave. During this time he found work at a market garden, and Hortham released him to the care of his mother.

A new competency assessment was scheduled when Straffen turned 21 and concluded that he should remain under supervision for a further five years. When his family appealed the decision, the supervision period was reduced to just six months.

John Straffen was 21-years-old with the mental capacity of a child of 10. He'd spent the last ten years in supervised care and although he had shown an occasional propensity for violence he'd been, in the main, a model inmate. The authorities had no way of knowing the tragedy he was about to unleash upon the unsuspecting community into which he was being released.

No one will ever know what turned John Straffen from a burglar who suffered occasional temper tantrums to the brutal murderer of three young girls. One theory is that it was Straffen's way of getting back at the authorities. Straffen had long been resentful of authority figures, particularly the police, whom he blamed for all the problems he'd had since his first arrest at the age of eight. At around the time of Straffen's release, the strangulation murder of a 7-year-old girl named Christine Butcher dominated the news. It has been suggested that Straffen followed the story, noted the problems the murder was causing for the police and decided to add to their headaches by strangling a few young girls himself. Far-fetched as that motive seems, it might well have made sense to a hulking 21-year-old with anger to spare and the mental capacity of a 10-year-old.

On July 15, 1951, Straffen was on his way to the cinema, when he encountered six-year-old Brenda Goddard gathering flowers in her front garden. He offered to show her a better place and led the little girl to a nearby field. After lifting Brenda over a fence he took her into a copse of trees where he strangled her. He then bashed her head against a tree. Then he casually walked to the cinema and watched the movie before returning home.

Although Straffen was not considered a violent offender, the Bath police knew of his history as a mental patient and decided to interview him about Brenda's disappearance. On July 31, they called on his place of work and questioned his employer about his movements. This resulted in Straffen being dismissed from his job. Then, on August 3, Straffen himself was pulled in, but stoically denied knowing Brenda. In a later interview with a prison psychiatrist, Straffen said that he did this to annoy the police, because he hated them.

Five days after he was questioned by police, Staffen was again at the cinema. The movie was Tarzan and The Jungle Queen. Also in the audience, that day was nine- year-old Cicely Batstone, who'd been allowed to go to the movie alone as a treat.

Straffen somehow befriended the girl and persuaded her to go with him by bus to another movie theater across town to see She Wore A Yellow Ribbon. Afterward, he convinced her to go with him to a meadow known locally as, 'Tumps.' There he strangled Cicely, leaving her body under a hedge.

Unlike in the murder of Brenda Goddard, a number of people had seen Straffen with the girl: a bus conductor had seen them traveling together; a courting couple had seen them crossing the meadow; and another woman, a policeman's wife, had seen them walking together near the field. When news of Cecily's disappearance broke the following morning she told her husband about the sighting. A search of the meadow soon turned up Cicely's body and the description of the man she'd been with soon led officers to Straffen's door.

Straffen was arrested on the morning of August 9. "Is it about the little girl I took to the pictures last night?" he asked the arresting officer. "When I left her she was dead under the hedge."

Then, without prompting, also confessed the murder of Brenda Goddard, saying: "She never screamed when I squeezed her neck, so I bashed her against a tree. I didn't feel sorry."

Straffen was charged with murder and remanded in custody on August 31, with a trial date set for October 17, 1951, at Taunton Assizes. However, only one witness would appear at the trial. Dr. Peter Parkes, the medical officer at Horfield Prison, testified to Straffen's medical history and stated his conclusion that Straffen was unfit to stand trial. Oliver commented that: "In this country, we do not try people who are insane. You might as well try a baby in arms. If a man cannot understand what is going on, he cannot be tried." The jury then formally returned a verdict that Straffen was insane and unfit to plead.

Straffen was sent to Broadmoor, a secure hospital for the criminally insane in Berkshire, to be held there indefinitely.

That should have been the end of the story, but unfortunately, Straffen would be given to opportunity to kill again. On 29 April 1952, Straffen and another patient were cleaning some outbuildings that stood close to the 10-foot high boundary wall. In a small yard immediately adjacent to the wall was a low shed with a sloping roof that was 8-foot-tall at its highest point. Straffen asked his supervisor if he could go into the yard to shake out his duster and was given permission to do so. Once inside, he climbed to the roof, scaled the wall and disappeared over the top. The escape had quite obviously been planned as he was wearing civilian clothes under his prison uniform.

Only 20 minutes after escaping, Straffen approached Doris Spencer who was working in her garden. He asked her for a drink of water and, as he drank, discussed with her the likelihood of escapes from Broadmoor. He left ten minutes later.

An hour and a half later he reached Farley Hill and at about five o'clock came across five-year-old Linda Bowyer riding her bicycle. No one knows what transpired between Linda and Straffen, but within half an hour the little girl was dead.

Straffen next showed up at the home of a Mrs. Kenyon, where he begged a cup of tea and persuaded the woman to give him a ride to the bus stop. As they were approaching the stop, Straffen saw some uniformed men and immediately bolted from the car and ran away. Kenyon then stopped and told the men (who were actually Broadmoor guards) of the suspicious behavior of her passenger and Straffen was recaptured a few minutes later. He'd been at liberty for less than four hours. As he was being driven back to the hospital Straffen told his captors: "I have finished with crime."

The body of Linda Bowyer was found the following morning and having heard that a Broadmoor patient had been on the loose at the time of the murder, police officers arrived at the hospital to interview Straffen. He immediately incriminated himself by stating (without being asked) "I did not kill her." The police officer told Straffen that no one had said that anyone had been killed, and Straffen then said: "I did not kill the little girl on the bicycle."

On May 1, Straffen was formally charged with the murder of Linda Bowyer, and moved from Broadmoor to the high-security Brixton Prison. His murder trial opened on July 21. Straffen's defense team pleaded him not guilty and opted to leave the question of his sanity up to the jury. This was a bad miscalculation. At the conclusion of the trial, the jury deliberated for less than an hour, before returning a verdict of guilty. Mr. Justice Cassels then sentenced Straffen to death.

Subsequent appeals were denied and the execution was scheduled for September 4, 1952. However, on August 29, it was announced that the Home Secretary, David Maxwell Fyfe, had recommended a reprieve.

Straffen would spend the next 55 years of his life behind bars. He died at Frankland Prison in County Durham on November 19, 2007, at the age of 77 years. At the time of his death, he was the longest-serving prisoner in British history.

Fred and Rosemary West

The House of Horrors Killers

"Behave or you'll end up under the patio like Heather." –
Fred West

Throughout the spring and summer of 1994, the world's media
flocked to Gloucester, to an ordinary three-story house at 25
Cromwell Street. There, as journalists from as far afield as
Australia and Japan waited, came revelations almost too gruesome
to comprehend, revelations of sexual perversion, torture, incest,
murder, and dismemberment.

It all began on the afternoon of Thursday, February 24. That
afternoon, police officers arrived at the home that Frederick West
shared with his wife Rosemary and their children. Fred was not
there when the police arrived, by the door was opened by his
sullen, heavy-set wife. The officers explained to Mrs. West why

they were there and she immediately placed a call to her husband, who was working at a house some 20 minutes drive away.

"You'd better get back home," she told Fred, "They're going to dig up the garden, looking for Heather."

Frederick Walter Stephen West was born on September 29, 1941, in the Herefordshire village of Much Marcle. His parents, Walter and Daisy were farm laborers, but despite their precarious financial situation, they had six children besides Fred, all of them born within a ten-year-period.

Walter West was a strict disciplinarian who (according to Fred) routinely committed incest with his daughters. "I made you so I'm entitled to have you," was an oft-spoken credo. Still, Fred admired his father and regarded him as a role model. His relationship with his mother was much closer. He was her favorite and she doted on him, often appearing at Fred's school to harangue teachers who disciplined him. These interventions, though, did Fred few favors. He became known as a "mamma's boy" and was the target of ruthless teasing by his peers.

Fred was not gifted academically but showed an aptitude for art and woodwork. When he left school at age 15, he was all but illiterate and took the only employment available to him - he became a farm laborer, like his parents.

With his somewhat simian looks, coarse hair and gap-toothed smile, Fred was far from handsome. Still, he appeared to be attractive to some girls and unfazed by rejection. By the age of sixteen, he was already extremely sexually aggressive, and would pursue any girl that caught his eye.

When Fred was seventeen, a serious motorcycle accident left him in a coma for a week and resulted in him having a metal plate inserted into his head. His leg was also fractured and was made permanently shorter than the other leg. The accident had another side effect; it made him prone to sudden fits of rage.

After recovering from the accident, Fred met a pretty 16-year-old named Catherine Bernadette Costello. Nicknamed Rena, Costello was an accomplished thief and a habitual liar. She and Fred hit it off immediately and were soon lovers, the relationship only ending when Rena returned to Scotland.

Fred soon turned his attentions to other targets. In one incident, he stuck his hand up a woman's skirt and she responded by lashing out at him, causing a fall down a fire escape that knocked him unconscious and resulted in another head injury. It has been speculated that this incident, along with the motorcycle accident, resulted in Fred suffering permanent brain damage.

By 1961, Fred West, now 20, was in and out of trouble with the police. First, he was arrested for stealing cigarette cases from a jewelry store. That resulted in a fine. Then he was accused of impregnating a 13-year-old girl, a friend of the West family. This latest scandal caused him to become estranged from his family, but at trial, his attorney managed to get him off, based on diminished responsibility due to the head injuries he'd suffered. He continued to steal from the construction site where he now worked and to pursue underage girls. When challenged about this, his usual response was: "Well, doesn't everyone do it?"

In 1962, at Daisy's urging, Fred was allowed to move back into the West family home. That summer, his old girlfriend, Rena Costello, returned from Scotland and the two immediately took up where they'd left off. Rena was only 17, but already had a record for prostitution and burglary. She was also pregnant, the result of a dalliance with a Pakistani bus driver.

None of this seemed to bother Fred. The couple married in secret in November 1962 and moved to Scotland. Rena's daughter, Charmaine, was born in March 1963. Because Fred's parents believed that Rena had been carrying Fred's child, he concocted a ridiculous story to account for Charmaine's ethnicity. He wrote to his mother and said that the baby had died at birth, and he and Rena had adopted a mixed-race child. The West family appears to have believed him.

Meanwhile, Fred had gotten a job driving an ice cream truck, something that suited him down to the ground. His easy line of chatter coupled with his apparent politeness and sincerity allowed him to seduce a number of the teenaged girls who flocked to his vehicle to buy ice cream.

In 1964, Rena bore Fred a daughter, who they named Anna Marie. Their marriage was far from tranquil and Rena often complained about Fred's persistent sexual demands. Still, she stayed, even bringing a friend of hers, Ann McFall, to live in their home. At around this time, Fred was involved in an accident with the ice cream truck that killed a four-year-old boy. Although he was cleared of any blame, he decided to move his family back to Gloucester. Ann McFall went with them.

Fred found a job in a slaughterhouse, something which many commentators believe had a profound affect on him. Surrounded every day by blood and carnage, he developed a morbid obsession with corpses and dismemberment. If Fred West's sexual perversion became slowly more obsessive after his marriage to Rena, then his desire to mutilate corpses began during the time he worked as a butcher.

The West's hadn't been in Gloucester long when cracks began to appear in their marriage. Rena wanted to take the children back to Scotland, but Fred refused, so Rena went alone. When she returned, in July 1966, she found Fred and Ann McFall living together with the children in a trailer.

At around this time, there were a number of sexual assaults in and around Gloucester, committed by a man matching Fred's description, although he was never charged or even questioned about any of the crimes.

In early 1967, Anna McFall became pregnant with Fred's child and began pressuring Fred to divorce Rena and marry her. Not long after, she disappeared. Years later it would emerge that Fred murdered Anna and buried her body in the woods near the trailer park. When the body was eventually found, it showed evidence that it had been ritually mutilated prior to burial. All of the fingers and toes had been removed, a signature that Fred West would repeat during his later crimes.

After Anna's disappearance, Rena moved into the trailer. Fred seems to have forgiven her for deserting him, but he required that Rena made a contribution to the household by going out to work as a prostitute. While Rena was thus engaged, Fred began turning his sexual attentions to his young adoptive daughter, Charmaine.

In January 1968, a pretty 15-year-old named Mary Bastholm was abducted from a bus stop in Gloucester. Fred West was never charged with the crime, but there are a number of reasons to believe that he was the man responsible. Mary worked at the Pop-In café, which Fred frequented, and also did some building work at. Mary had been seen in the company of Fred's former lover, Anna McFall, and had also been seen by a witness in Fred's car. Given the sexual assaults on other young women in the area, it is not a stretch to imagine that Fred might have been responsible for Mary's disappearance.

In February 1968, Daisy West died from complications caused by a gallbladder operation. Fred had been close to his mother, and her death hit him hard. Still, in November of that year, he would meet the woman who'd play an even more important role in his life, Rosemary Letts.

Rosemary Letts was born on November 29, 1953, in Devon, England. The Letts family was plagued by mental problems. Rose's father, Bill, was a schizophrenic, while her mother, Daisy, suffered from severe depression. Bill Letts was a violent, abusive man, not averse to using his fists on his wife and children. He is also believed to have sexually abused his daughters.

As if this wasn't enough, Rose had another strike against her, even before she was born. While pregnant, Daisy had undergone electroshock therapy to deal with her depression. Whether this affected Rose or not is unknown, but she was certainly different to other children.

As a baby, she'd rock herself obsessively in her cot, a habit she carried into childhood when she'd sit nodding her head for hours on end. It also soon became clear that she was a bit "slow." At school, they called her, "Dozy Rosie," reflecting her inability to grasp even simple concepts. What she lacked in intelligence, though, she made up for in guile. She was particularly manipulative when it came to her father. She was his favorite and thus escaped the savage beatings meted out to her siblings.

Rose was a pretty girl, with big, dark eyes, and long brown hair. As she got older, though, she put on weight, making her the butt of cruel jokes at school. But her peers knew to tease her from a safe distance. She had a vicious temper and attacked anyone who taunted her.

As she reached her teens, Rose showed signs of being sexually precocious and, because he father forbade her dating boys her own age, she turned her attention to older men. Jim Tyler, Rose's brother-in-law would later claim that the teenaged Rose had a number of older lovers, and even tried to seduce him on one occasion. There were also, of course, rumors that Rose was involved in a sexual relationship with her own father.

Thus, by 1969, Rose Letts was going nowhere fast. She was uneducated, bad-tempered and not very quick-witted. Her primary interest seemed to be in seducing older men. Her prospects were bleak. And then she met Fred West.

Bill Letts, perhaps seeing Fred as a rival for Rose's affections, was initially dead- set against the relationship. When he found that Rose was sleeping with Fred, he first reported the matter to Social Services and then threatened to beat Fred up. Neither of these measures was effective in separating the pair. When Rose did eventually go back to live with her father, it was because Fred had been sent to prison for various petty thefts. By then, she was already pregnant with Fred's child.

Then, after Fred was released, Rose went to live in his trailer and became a de facto stepmother to Charmaine and Anna Marie. In 1970, she gave birth to a daughter, who she and Fred named Heather.

Three young children would be a handful for any young mother to cope with, let alone a 16-year-old with anger management problems. Neither was Fred much help. He was in and out of prison and when he was home, he was unable to find work. Making ends meet was a constant struggle, leaving Rose in a perpetual bad mood. She took her frustrations out on the children, especially Rena's offspring, Charmaine and Anna Marie.

Then, in the summer of 1971, Fred returned from his latest term of incarceration to find Charmaine gone. Rose said that Rena had come to get her, but the truth was much more sinister. Charmaine's body would be recovered some 20 years later, buried under the kitchen floor at Midland Road where the Wests lived prior to their move to Cromwell Street. The body carried Fred West's signature, with the fingers, toes and kneecaps removed. It can, therefore, be assumed that Rose eventually broke down and admitted to Fred that she'd killed Charmaine and that he'd then buried the body. It was a secret he'd hold over Rose for the rest of her life.

But Rose had created a problem for Fred to deal with. What happened when Rena came looking for her daughter? That problem was resolved in August 1971, when, as expected Rena came to take her daughter away. Fred evaded her initial questions then got her drunk and strangled her. He then dismembered her body (including the characteristic mutilation of fingers and toes) and buried her remains in a field, not far from where he'd disposed of Ann McFall.

Later that year, Fred and Rose befriended their new neighbor, Elizabeth Agius, who babysat for them several times. Fred was attracted to the young woman and openly propositioned her. A shocked Elizabeth turned him down, but Fred would eventually get his way. After drugging Elizabeth, he raped her. She was too terrified and ashamed to report the incident.

Fred and Rose married at the Gloucester Registry Office in January 1972 and in July, Rose bore him another daughter, Mae. But their marriage was an unconventional one. Rose, with Fred's encouragement, ran a prostitution business out of their home, catering especially to West Indian men. This was more than just a source of extra income. Among his many perversions, Fred enjoyed voyeurism and liked to watch the action through a peephole.

In mid-1972, the couple moved their growing family to number 25 Cromwell Street. The house looked slightly run down from the outside but was large, with a garage and a good-sized cellar. Fred particularly liked the cellar. He told Elizabeth Agius (only half-jokingly) that he planned on turning it into a torture chamber.

Not long after, he committed his first atrocity down there, raping his eight-year-old daughter, Anna Marie, while Rose held her down. The little girl was in so much pain that she had to stay home from school for several days after. She was threatened with violence if she ever told anyone.

In late 1972, Fred and Rose hired 17-year-old girl Caroline Roberts as a nanny. Caroline was very pretty, and both Rose and Fred soon tried to seduce her, resulting in her leaving the post. However, on December 6, 1972, the Wests invited her to their home. Caroline was fond of the children and so she agreed. Once there, she was overpowered, stripped and raped. Fred then threatened her not to tell anyone or, "I'll keep you in the cellar and let my black friends have you, and when we're finished we'll kill you and bury you under the paving stones."

Terrified, Caroline agreed not to say anything. However, when her mother saw the bruises on her body, she got the truth from her and went to the police. A hearing was scheduled for January 1973, but Fred was able to convince the magistrate that Caroline had been a willing participant. The charge was reduced to indecent assault and the Wests walked away with a paltry fine each.

Still, Caroline was lucky, the next woman to stay at 25 Cromwell Street would not get out alive. Lynda Gough was a seamstress who moved in to help care for the children and disappeared around April 1973. She would later be found buried under the garage. When Lynda's mother came looking for her, she found Rose West wearing Lynda's clothes, but the Wests insisted that Lynda had moved on, to take up a job in Weston-super-Mare.

August 1973 saw the birth of the couple's first son, Stephen. In November that year, Fred and Rose abducted 15-year-old Carol Ann Cooper as she walked home from the cinema. The girl was held as a plaything for the sexually depraved couple, then snuffed out when she'd outlived her entertainment value. Her remains were added to the growing boneyard underneath 25 Cromwell Street.

A little over a month later, on December 27, university student Lucy Partington went missing after visiting a friend. Lucy left to catch a bus at around 10 p.m. and was never seen alive again. Like Carol Ann Cooper, she was sexually tortured for several days, then murdered, dismembered and incarcerated in a shallow grave. A week after she disappeared, Fred West went to a hospital in the early hours of the morning with a serious cut to his hand. It is believed that he cut himself while dismembering Lucy.

Lucy, like Carol Ann Cooper, was reported missing, but there was nothing to connect either of the girls to Fred and Rose. The Wests were at liberty to continue their killing spree.

Between April of 1974 and April of 1975, three more young women -- Therese Siegenthaler, 21, Shirley Hubbard, 15, and Juanita Mott, 18, were tortured and killed, their dismembered remains buried under the cellar floor at 25 Cromwell Street.

When found, their bodies bore witness to the suffering and indignity they'd been subjected to. Shirley's head had been wrapped entirely in tape with a plastic tube inserted into her nose so that she could breathe. Juanita was trussed in such a way that it appeared she'd been suspended from the beams on the cellar ceiling.

In 1976, the Wests lured an underage girl (identified only as Miss A during her court testimony) from a home for wayward girls. Miss A was taken to the cellar, where two naked girls were being held prisoner. She was forced to watch the girls being tortured and then raped by Fred and sexually assaulted by Rose. From her description, it seems one of the girls was Fred's daughter, Anna Marie, a constant target of the couple's sexual perversions. Fred would also allow Rosemary's clients to rape his adolescent daughter.

In 1977, the upstairs of the house was remodeled and the Wests took on a number of lodgers. One of them was Shirley Robinson, an 18-year-old former prostitute who became involved in sexual relationships with both Fred and Rose. Shirley became pregnant with Fred's child, while Rose was pregnant by one of her black clients.

Fred seemed delighted at the idea of Rose carrying a mixed-race child, but Rose was less thrilled with Shirley being pregnant by Fred. Then Shirley signed her own death warrant by foolishly trying to displace Rose in Fred's affections. She was killed in May 1978 and buried in the back garden along with her unborn baby. By that time, Rose had given birth to another daughter, Tara.

In November 1978, Rose and Fred had yet another daughter who they named Louise. Fred also impregnated his 14-year-old daughter, Anna Marie, but the pregnancy was ectopic and had to be terminated.

Rose's father died of a lung ailment in May 1979. Three months later, the Wests kidnapped a troubled teenager named Alison Chambers. After they raped and tortured her, Alison was killed and dismembered. She ended up beside Shirley Robinson in the rear garden.

In 1980, Anna Marie left home to live with her boyfriend, and Fred transferred his incestuous attention to Heather and Mae. When Heather resisted, she was viciously beaten. In June of that year, Rose gave birth to Barry, Fred's second son. There was another addition to the family in April 1982, although Rosemary Junior wasn't Fred's, she was mixed-race, as was Lucyanna, born July 1983.

All of these children in the household placed additional stress on Rose who became moody and increasingly violent, beating the kids at the slightest provocation. It is not known whether the Wests continued killing during this time. If they did, the bodies were not buried at number 25 Cromwell Street.

However, Fred continued to sexually abuse his daughters and continued to threaten them with dire consequence if they told anybody. The wall of silence held until 1986 when Heather told a friend. Unfortunately, the friend repeated the story to her parents who were friends of Fred and Rose. Once Fred got to hear of it, Heather's life was in jeopardy.

It has never been clearly established whether it was Fred or Rose who killed Heather. Fred would later confess to the murder but claim it was accidental. However, on the day following Heather's disappearance, Rose reportedly told a neighbor that she and Heather had had "a hell of a row," suggesting that she had perhaps initiated the attack on Heather.

After Heather's disappearance, Fred and Rose told their other children that Heather had left for a job in Devon. Later, they changed their story, claiming she'd run off with a lesbian lover. Later still, Fred would threaten the children that they would "end up under the patio like Heather" if they misbehaved.

The West's veil of silence would again be breached in May 1992, when he raped another of his daughters. The girl told a friend, who told her mother, who reported the matter to the police on August 4.

The matter was assigned to veteran Detective Constable Hazel
Savage. Fred West was well known to Detective Savage, who was
familiar with his many crimes and misdemeanors. She also
remembered his former wife Rena telling her stories about Fred's
sexual perversions.

On August 6, 1992, police arrived at 25 Cromwell Street with a
search warrant to look for pornography and evidence of child
abuse. The evidence they found there led to Fred being arrested
for rape and sodomy of a minor. Rose was arrested for assisting in
the rape.

Hazel Savage then started questioning the other members of the
family and began learning the shocking truth about the years of
abuse the West children had suffered. From Anna Marie, she
learned of the disappearances of Charmaine, Rena and Heather,
and of the oft-repeated threat of joining Heather under the patio.

The younger West children were taken into government care,
while Fred was held in custody pending trial and Rose remained
free on bail. Det. Savage meanwhile had launched a search for
Heather. The early results didn't look promising. Tax records
showed that Heather had not been employed in four years.
Medical insurance records showed that she hadn't visited a doctor
in that period. Either she had left the country or she was dead.

In the meantime, the rape case against the Wests was falling apart
as their children refused to testify against them. It seemed that

Fred and Rose would walk away scot-free. And they might well have done so, but for the persistence of Hazel Savage.

With the failure to find any trace of the missing girl, Det. Savage was beginning to fear that perhaps the rumors were true after all, that perhaps Heather was buried under the patio. The West children were re-questioned and repeated the threat that their father had made, that they'd "end up under the patio like Heather." It was enough for the police to obtain a search warrant.

On 24 February 1994, officers began searching the house and excavating the garden. They recovered the first human remains in the garden the following day. Fred West was taken into custody and immediately confessed to the murder of Heather. He then retracted before confessing again. One thing was constant throughout, though – he insisted that Rose wasn't involved.

By now it was clear that more than one body was buried at 25 Cromwell Street and faced with the mounting evidence against him West confessed to nine more murders, including that of his first wife Rena. Rosemary West remained at liberty until April 1994 when, despite Fred's continued protestations as to her innocence, she too was charged.

Fred and Rosemary West were brought before a Gloucester magistrate on June 30, 1994; he was charged with 11 murders, she with 10. Another charge was added to Fred's docket on July 3 after the body of Ann McFall was recovered.

But Fred West would never stand trial for his crimes. On January 1, 1995, he hanged himself in his cell at Winson Green Prison, Birmingham.

Rosemary West went on trial at Winchester Crown Court in 1995. She was found guilty on each of 10 counts of murder and sentenced to life imprisonment. The trial judge recommended that she should never be released and that decision was later ratified by the Home Secretary, meaning Rosemary West will die in prison.

Bible John

Glasgow, Scotland's largest city and economic heartbeat, has produced its fair share of villains. From Madeleine Smith who poisoned her lover in 1857 and was acquitted under the unique Scottish verdict of Not Proven, to Dr. Edward William Pritchard who committed a similar crime on his wife in 1865 and was the last man to be publically executed in Scotland; from the homicidal butler, Archibald Hall, to the notorious serial killer Peter Manuel, slayer of eight people in a murderous spree during the fifties. And then there's Ian Brady, born in Glasgow, who gained infamy for the horrendous Moors Murders.

But one serial killer, largely unknown outside Scotland, has entered the realm of Glasgow folklore, someone that Glaswegian parents still use as a bogeyman to get children to behave. He is Bible John, a still unidentified serial killer who terrorized the city during the late 1960's.

The fiend made his public debut on the night of February 22, 1968. Patricia Docker was a young nurse, the mother of a young toddler, whose husband was a Royal Air Force corporal stationed in England. On that Thursday evening some of Patricia's friends were going to the over 25's night at the Barrowland Ballroom, one of Glasgow's popular nightspots. They persuaded her to join them for a night of dancing and fun. Patricia's parents encouraged her to go along, she worked so hard after all, she could do with letting her hair down for an evening.

Leaving her young son in the care of his grandparents Patricia set off for the nightclub, stopping off first at another dancehall, the Majestic. Few people remember seeing Patricia at the Barrowland that evening. Some witnesses later recalled seeing her at both dancehalls, but couldn't say who she spoke to or who her dance partners might have been. However, more than one witness did recall that she left in the company of a young man.

The following morning, Friday the 23rd, a man on his way to work noticed something lying at the side of a quiet lane on his route. On closer examination, he was horrified to find it was the naked body of a young woman. The man ran immediately to call the police.

Officers arriving at the scene soon determined that the woman had been strangled with her own pantyhose and had been dead for several hours. An autopsy would later reveal that she'd also been raped. The police began searching the immediate area for the woman's clothing and other effects. But their efforts turned up nothing, leaving them to theorize that she had been killed somewhere else before being dumped in the lane.

By now, a crowd had gathered and someone was able to identify the victim. She was Patricia Docker they said, she lived close by. The bystander then ran to call Patricia's parents who were faced with the unenviable task of identifying their daughter's body, which had been left just yards away from their house.

While the police canvassed the neighborhood, they also continued their search for Patricia's clothes and handbag, even sending divers into the icy waters of the nearby River Cart. They found nothing, although the bag would later be retrieved from the River Clyde, suggesting that the killer was from that part of the city.

Neither did questioning the neighbors provide many answers. One woman did say that she'd heard cries in the early morning hours, but the information was too vague to be of use. A photograph of a policewoman of similar stature to Patricia, and wearing similar clothes, was circulated in the hope was that it might stir someone's memory. It too, led nowhere. Before long the trail had gone cold.

A year and a half passed and the brutal murder of Patricia Docker had faded from the memory of most Glaswegians when the killer struck again.

On the evening of August 16, 1969, Jemima McDonald, a 32-year-old mother of three, was looking forward to an evening out. With her sister, Margaret, babysitting her kids for the evening, Jemima headed for the Barrowland. As was common with young women of the day, she wore her hair in curlers under a scarf. On arriving at the club, she immediately headed for the bathroom where she removed the curlers and freshened up her makeup before making for the dance floor.

Jemima danced almost exclusively with one partner that night, a tall, fair-haired man in his late 20s or early 30s, wearing a blue suit. The couple was seen together in the early hours of the following morning, walking away from the dancehall.

Margaret was perplexed when her sister didn't show up to collect her children by the morning of August 17. But as the day wore on, she became more and more concerned. Later that day Margaret heard talk in the neighborhood about a body that some kids had discovered in an old tenement building in nearby MacKeith Street. Fearing the worst, she walked to the building where she made a grisly discovery.

Unlike Patricia, Jemima was fully clothed. However, like the earlier victim, she had been strangled with her own nylons and her handbag was missing from the scene. She'd also been beaten and raped. As the police began looking into similarities between the two homicides they discovered another connection. Both Patricia and Jemima had been menstruating at the time they were killed.

With not much evidence discovered at the crime scene, the police moved on to their next priority, questioning those who'd been at the Barrowland on the night Jemima was killed. When this failed to turn up any useful leads, they staged a re-enactment. A policewoman who resembled Jemima was dressed in similar clothing and retraced Jemima's last known steps. This yielded a few clues but got the police no closer to identifying a particular suspect.

They did, however, have a description of the man who'd been in Jemima's company that evening. A rough sketch was created and circulated to the media, the first time this had ever occurred in a Scottish murder investigation - sketches of suspects had previously been for police use only.

Meanwhile, Jemima's six siblings offered a reward of £100 for information leading to an arrest. This too, produced no tangible results.

The elusive killer had waited 18 months between the murders of Patricia Docker and Jemima McDonald. He'd wait just two months before claiming his next victim.

On Oct. 30, 1969, 20-year-old Helen Puttock was planning an evening out at the Barrowland Ballroom with her sister, Jean. Her husband offered to stay home to look after their two young boys, but he warned his wife to be careful. The murder of Jemima McDonald was still fresh in the public's mind. Helen scoffed at his concerns. She and Jean would be together all night, she was confident they would be safe.

During the evening, Helen began dancing with a tall, young man and, according to Jean's later testimony, the two spent much of the evening in each other's company. At around midnight, Helen told her new friend that she and Jean had to leave. He offered to see them home in a taxi.

The police would later question Jean extensively about the short cab ride. She said that the man seemed to resent her presence and had addressed himself solely to Helen during the cab ride. However, she had learned that the man's name was John Templeton or Sempleson, that he had a sister and had been raised in a strict religious household and was adept at quoting passages of scripture. He spoke disparagingly of the sort of women who frequented places like the Barrowland, calling the dancehall a "den of iniquity." Somewhere during the conversation, John had also mentioned that he had a cousin who had recently hit a hole-in-one while playing golf.

When the cab had dropped Jean off at her house in Knightswood, John had not even bothered to acknowledge her as she said goodbye. As the cab pulled away from the curb, Jean had no idea that it would be the last time she saw her sister.

The following morning, Helen's body was discovered in the back garden of her flat in Earl Street, Scotstoun. As with the previous victims, she'd been strangled with her own pantyhose and her handbag had been taken. She had also been having her period, and the killer had removed her sanitary napkin and placed it in one of her armpits. An autopsy would show that she'd been raped, but unlike in the other crimes, the killer had left a couple of clues; a bite mark on the victim's leg and a semen stain on her clothing. These did not help police at the time, but would come into play decades later.

As the police launched a massive investigation, one of the biggest in Scottish history, the press picked up on the killer's apparent ability to quote scripture and gave him a nickname that would haunt Glasgow for decades to come: "Bible John."

But who was Bible John? Did he even exist or was he purely a media creation. At least one of the lead investigators on the case believed that the murders were unconnected and unlikely to have been committed by the same man. This is a startling viewpoint given the similarities between the crimes; all of the victims had spent the last night of their lives at the Barrowland Ballroom; all three were strangled with their own nylons; each of the bodies was left in close proximity to the victim's home; the handbags of all three victims were carried away by the killer; all three victims were menstruating at the time of their deaths. Victims two and three had been in the company of a tall, fair-haired man. It seems highly unlikely that they were unconnected.

Over 100 officers were now working the case, collecting more than 50, 000 statements, questioning bus and taxi drivers, even going undercover at the Barrowland. A color sketch of the man seen with both Jemima and Helen was released, while the BBC screened a recreation of Helen's last known movements. Jean's description led police to focus part of their investigation on the armed forces, as Bible John's short haircut may have indicated that he was serving in the military.

Additionally, the police began questioned dentists about male patients who had the overlapping tooth that Jean had described. And the police even visited golf courses, up and down the country, to check on John's story about his cousin's hole-in-one.

Meanwhile, a Glasgow newspaper brought in a renowned Dutch psychic, and a local psychiatrist produced a profile of sorts, describing Bible John as friendly, but somewhat prudish with an interest in subjects ranging from the Third Reich to sorcery. Helen's husband even put up a reward for information, amounting to his entire life's savings. It was all to no avail. Over the years, Jean would pay over 250 visits to view suspects that matched her description. None of them was Bible John.

Time passed, and with no arrest or even progress to report the
case began to fade from the public eye. In 1977, a murder that
bore some of the hallmarks of the Bible John murders briefly
stirred renewed interest in the case.

In 1983, a wealthy Glaswegian hired a private detective to track
down a childhood friend whom he thought resembled an artist's
depiction of Bible John. The investigators found the man in
question living in Holland. He was questioned but quickly cleared
of any involvement.

But the police were not without suspects, and one, in particular,
stood out. The man, known as John McInnes, bore an uncanny
resemblance to the police sketch. Even after he committed suicide
in 1980, he continued to be considered a prime suspect.

By the late 1990s, DNA technology allowed the police to revisit the
evidence, in particular, the semen left on Helen's clothing. In
February 1996, Marie Cassidy of Glasgow University supervised
the exhumation of John McInnes's body and took DNA samples for
comparison to the evidence. The results proved conclusively that
John McInnes was not Bible John.

Another possible suspect was the serial killer Peter Tobin,
convicted in 2007 of the murder of student Angelika Kluk. Tobin
had lived in Glasgow at the time of the Bible John murders and
bore a strong resemblance to the suspect. He was also a regular at
the Barrowland, and at least one woman testified that she had
been raped by Tobin after meeting him at the dancehall. There are

other pieces of circumstantial evidence that point to Tobin as well. All three of his former wives testified that they had been strangled and raped by him. They also said that Tobin was often driven to violence by the menstrual cycle, something which has long been considered the motive behind the Bible John murders. Tobin was also a staunch Roman Catholic with strong religious views.

A DNA comparison could have proven conclusively whether Tobin was Bible John or no, but unfortunately, the DNA evidence had become degraded by the time of his arrest, making such a comparison impossible.

We will likely never know who Bible John was.

For more True Crime books by Robert Keller please visit

http://bit.ly/kellerbooks

19411054R00095

Printed in Great Britain
by Amazon